Jane's Patisserie

Jane's Patisserie

Deliciously customisable cakes,
bakes and treats

JANE DUNN

EBURY
PRESS

INTRODUCTION

I'm Jane and I am the foodie, blogger and baker behind the blog Jane's Patisserie. I have always adored cooking, baking and anything to do with food, and creating this book for you has been an absolute dream.

Ever since I was little, I have loved baking… Apparently, I got it from my gran who also adored it. My mum tells me that I loved watching my gran make my first birthday cake and, even though I can't remember it, maybe that's where it all started! Growing up, I enjoyed the fun lessons on cooking in junior school, and when there was a bake sale I was always one of the first to put my name down as a baker. I never thought I was particularly good at it, but I just completely and utterly loved it!

When I went to secondary school, I found my love for designing things and all things arty so, when I started baking and cooking a bit more when I was at college, I was able to put those two things together. Getting to create bakes, planning decorations, and playing around with new ideas and flavours gave me confidence, and it soon became a passion. This made me wonder if cooking and baking was something I wanted to pursue as a career, and I am so glad I did!

After college, I started training at cookery school and really enjoyed the patisserie element of my course which inspired me to start my blog – www.janespatisserie.com. I wanted to start a blog that could become my creative space, somewhere to share my love for everything sweet. At first, I just blogged about what I made. I would take a few photos and post the recipe, not expecting anyone to actually make the recipes I was writing!

Things have changed quite a bit since then, I now have millions of blog views every month, thousands upon thousands of followers and the ability to work for myself, and I can't thank my followers enough for that opportunity. I now have hundreds of recipes, covering all kinds of bakes, and I love nothing more than getting started on a new creation – well, maybe the first bite when it's done! I love to write recipes that anyone can bake. My recipes are designed to be easy, suitable for all levels of bakers, and something that you can make with your friends or family and enjoy sharing.

As you can imagine, the kitchen is my favourite room in the house, my happy place. I always gravitate towards it and I spend most days in there experimenting with new flavours and recipes that I know my readers will adore.

My hope is that this book can be your go-to for the special occasion bakes, for the bake sales, or just for that special something you crave. I've made sure that every one of the recipes in this book is customisable, and I've included simple tips to give you a little inspiration on how you can make each recipe your own. I want this book to give you the confidence to experiment and create bakes that make you and anyone you share them with smile! And remember, if your experiments don't always go to plan, don't worry – baking is all about having fun and spreading a little joy!

Baking is a science, but that doesn't mean that it has to be complicated. Most of my recipes start from a basic recipe or just a few simple ingredients that can be customised and adapted to suit you. I love coming back to those iconic flavour combinations – white chocolate and raspberry, chocolate and orange, coffee and walnuts – but there are so many more for you to explore.

As you go through the book, you'll see that I've included a mix of the most popular recipes on my blog and brand-new exclusive recipes requested by my wonderful followers – look out for this symbol ♥ and you might find just what you've been asking for! I hope this book inspires you to bake something you love, to enjoy with those you love.

Happy baking!

Jane x

BAKER'S NOTES

USEFUL EQUIPMENT

You don't need a fully kitted out kitchen to make delicious bakes, but there are a few essentials you'll need to get started, such as a decent set of weighing scales (to convert my measurements to imperial please see the conversion chart on page 221). These are my top pieces of equipment.

- Weighing scales
- Measuring spoons
- Baking trays
- Cake tins
- Parchment paper
- Oven thermometer
- Timer
- Mixing bowls
- Rubber spatulas
- Hand whisks
- Sieve

- Stand mixer
- Electric hand whisk
- Food processor
- Large and small piping bags
- Piping nozzles
- Offset spatula
- Cake scraper
- Cookie scoop
- Rolling pin
- Clingfilm

USEFUL INGREDIENTS

I have a pretty well stocked baking cupboard and it really helps me to experiment with new ideas. If you are looking to stock up, these are the most useful ingredients to have at home.

- Plain flour
- Self-raising flour
- Strong white bread flour
- Cornflour
- Cocoa powder
- Yeast
- Baking powder
- Bicarbonate of soda

- Powdered gelatine
- White granulated sugar
- Caster sugar
- Soft light/dark brown sugar
- Icing sugar
- Unsalted butter
- Baking spread
- Full-fat milk
- Full-fat soft cheese
- Eggs
- Oils
- Vanilla extract
- Ground spices
- Food colourings

- Dark chocolate (70% cocoa solids)
- Milk chocolate
- White chocolate
- Salt
- Sprinkles
- Jams/preserves
- Nuts
- Dried fruits
- Fresh and frozen fruits
- Condensed milk
- A supply of your favourite chocolates and biscuits!

INGREDIENT GUIDE

BUTTER:
Use unsalted block butter or a baking spread (I use Stork) for baking cakes, cookie bars, brownies etc. When you are decorating cakes, however, it is important to use block butter as spread is too soft.

SUGAR:
In cookies, I prefer to use granulated or soft light brown sugars, or a combination of both. Generally, I prefer not to use caster sugar in cookies. In cakes I use caster sugar or soft light brown sugar. In cheesecakes, you can use caster sugar instead of icing sugar if you prefer.

EGGS:
All eggs used in the recipes are medium, unless otherwise stated. I also always use free-range eggs, and organic where possible.

VANILLA:
The best types of vanilla to use are extract, bean paste, or pods. I don't tend to use vanilla essence as it is artificial.

CHOCOLATE:
For dark chocolate I recommend using one with a cocoa solids content of 70% or higher. You can use cooking chocolate in any recipe, but supermarket own brands are just as good too.

SOFT CHEESE:
When making a cheesecake, or anything using a soft cream cheese, it is important to use full-fat. The fat content is what helps make the cheesecakes set. You can also use mascarpone instead of soft cream cheese.

FLOUR:
In most of my recipes I use plain flour (for cookies, crumble toppings etc.) or self-raising flour (for cakes). You can make your own self-raising flour by whisking 2 level teaspoons of baking powder into 150g plain flour. However, if you use self-raising flour instead of plain flour, what you make will have a different texture due to the raising agents.

RAISING AGENTS:
Baking powder and bicarbonate of soda are different ingredients and should not be treated in the same way. When following a recipe, make sure you use the type listed, or the correct measurements.

BISCUITS:
Generally, I use plain digestive biscuit when making a biscuit base, such as for a cheesecake. You can use a chocolate coated biscuit, or a filled biscuit instead, but you will need to reduce the butter content by at least one-third.

FOOD COLOURING:
I prefer to use specialist cake decorating colours that are usually best bought online. Liquid food colours are not strong enough, and often result in an odd taste in recipes. Oil-based colours are best for mixing in with melted chocolate.

Cheese
CAKES

This chapter is probably my favourite. I honestly adore every recipe in this book but if you have followed my blog for a while, you know that cheesecake is one of my favourite things. When you break it down, most no-bake cheesecakes are a simple mix of five ingredients and that's what I love about them. Biscuits, butter, soft cheese, sugar, cream, and you're ready to go!

Baked cheesecakes do take a little more work; they have a firmer texture and are similar to the classic New York-style cheesecake. These are just as delicious as no-bake cheesecakes, and are a great option if you have the extra time to bake. Whether you are following a baked or no-bake recipe, both need to be in the fridge for a while before you can tuck in and enjoy them. It's okay though, they are 100 per cent worth the wait.

Cheesecakes can be made with basically any flavour you can think of, but in this chapter you'll find 12 delicious examples of my favourites: no-bake, baked, fruity, chocolatey and more. Enjoy!

The main ingredients I use (to make a cheesecake to serve 12) are:

- 300g biscuits
- 100—150g unsalted butter
- 500g full-fat soft cheese
- 300ml double cream
- 100g sugar (I tend to use icing sugar but you can use caster sugar too)

MY TOP TIPS FOR CHEESCAKES:

1 I find springform cake tins are the easiest to use as it makes it easier to get the cheesecake out at the end! Crush your biscuits to a fine crumb, mix with the melted butter and then press into the base of the tin in an even layer.

2 For the cheesecake mix, I use a stand mixer or an electric whisk to speed the process up, but it can be done by hand. You just need to make sure the mixture is smooth.

3 When adding the cream, I like to add mine as liquid and whisk it up in the bowl with the soft cheese and sugar – less washing up is always a plus! If you're working by hand, without an electric whisk, then you can always whip the cream separately and fold it into the main mixture once it's whipped.

4 When you add the finished mix to the tin to set, you'll need to make sure you've packed it in at the sides to prevent any air gaps and that the top is smooth. I find an offset spatula or a scraper the easiest tool to use.

NO-BAKE MILLIONAIRE'S CHEESECAKE

Serves: 12

Prep: 45 minutes
Set: 6+ hours
Lasts: 3+ days, in the fridge

BASE:
300g shortbread biscuits
75g unsalted butter, melted

CARAMEL:
375g condensed milk
150g unsalted butter
150g soft light brown sugar

CHOCOLATE CHEESECAKE FILLING:
250g milk chocolate, broken into chunks
500g full-fat soft cheese
1 tsp vanilla extract
100g icing sugar
300ml double cream

DECORATION (OPTIONAL):
12 mini millionaire's shortbread bites
Chocolate curls
Shortbread crumbs

A recipe to combine a few of my favourite things… biscuits, caramel and cheesecake. Slightly more effort is required with this cheesecake, but it's not as scary as it sounds. The biscuit is base is like any other, and the soft and chewy caramel is deceptively easy but does give an extra layer of flavour to the recipe. The chocolate cheesecake filling I use is sweet, but can be made with whatever chocolate flavour you like, and the shop-bought millionaire's bites to decorate finish the cheesecake off perfectly.

BASE:
Blitz the shortbread biscuits to a fine crumb in a food processor, or bash with a rolling pin in a bowl. Mix in the melted butter until combined. Press the mixture into the bottom of a deep, 20cm springform cake tin and refrigerate while you make the caramel.

CARAMEL:
Put all the caramel ingredients into a large heavy-based pan and melt together over a low heat until smooth. Once melted, turn the heat up until the mixture starts to boil. Continue to boil the mixture for 2½ minutes, stirring constantly so the mixture does not catch and burn on the bottom. Pour the caramel onto the biscuit base and return to the fridge while you make the filling.

CHOCOLATE CHEESECAKE FILLING:
Put the chocolate into a clean heatproof bowl and melt until smooth – I usually do this in 30-second bursts in the microwave but you can also set the bowl over a pan of simmering water over a low heat (bain-marie). Leave the chocolate to cool for 5 minutes.

In a large bowl, add the soft cheese, vanilla extract and icing sugar and whisk until smooth. Pour in the melted chocolate and whisk again until smooth. Finally pour in the double cream and whisk again until thick. (Alternatively, whip the cream separately and then fold through the cream

cheese and chocolate mix.) Once thickened, reserve 2–3 heaped tablespoons of the mixture and spread the rest on top of the caramel layer.

DECORATION:

Use the leftover mixture to pipe 12 swirls on top of the cheesecake and then add a mini shortbread bite to each one. Finish by sprinkling over some chocolate curls and shortbread crumbs. Leave the cheesecake to set in the fridge for at least 6 hours, or preferably overnight.

Once set, remove from the tin and serve!

CUSTOMISE:

The caramel can be made with caster sugar for a lighter flavour and colour, or soft dark brown sugar for a deeper treacle flavour.

The biscuit base can be made with digestives, or even flavoured with 25g cocoa powder added to the biscuits when mixing.

NO-BAKE CHOCOLATE ORANGE CHEESECAKE

Serves: 12

Prep: 30 minutes
Set: 6+ hours
Lasts: 3+ days, in the fridge

BASE:
300g digestive biscuits
100g unsalted butter, melted

FILLING:
300g milk chocolate, broken into chunks
500g full-fat soft cheese
75g icing sugar
1 tsp orange extract or zest of 1 orange
300ml double cream

DECORATION (OPTIONAL):
50g chocolate, melted
150ml double cream
2 tbsp icing sugar
Sprinkles
Grated chocolate
Orange zest
Chocolate chunks

CUSTOMISE:
Make this easier by using chocolate that is already flavoured with orange!

You can also completely change up the citrus flavours… white chocolate and lemon, dark chocolate and orange, dark chocolate and lime – or anything you fancy.

Chocolate and orange together is one of the best flavours in the world. The classic combination is milk chocolate with orange, but I find it works well with dark chocolate and white chocolate as well. This recipe is great at Christmas time, but I will happily eat it year-round, and have even made it for myself for my birthday before! The recipe has been a fan-favourite on my blog for so many years now that it definitely needed a place in this book!

Blitz the biscuits to a fine crumb in a food processor, or bash with a rolling pin in a bowl. Mix the melted butter with the biscuits until combined, then press the mixture into the bottom of a deep, 20cm springform cake tin and refrigerate while you prepare the filling.

Melt your milk chocolate until smooth – I do this in a heatproof bowl in the microwave in 30-second bursts, but you can also do it in a bowl set over a pan of simmering water (bain-marie). Leave the chocolate to cool for 5–10 minutes.

In a separate bowl, add the soft cheese, icing sugar and orange extract or orange zest and whisk until smooth. Add your melted and cooled chocolate and whisk again until smooth.

Pour in the double cream and whisk again. (Alternatively, you can whip the cream separately to soft peaks, and then fold through the cream cheese/chocolate mix.) Once the mixture has thickened, spread the mixture evenly over the biscuit base. Leave to set in the fridge for at least 6 hours, or preferably overnight.

Once set, carefully remove the cheesecake from the tin. Drizzle over some melted chocolate – you can use a small spoon, or a piping bag. Whip the cream and icing sugar together and then use this mixture to pipe swirls onto your cheesecake. Finally, decorate with sprinkles, grated chocolate, orange zest and chunks of chocolate.

NO-BAKE WHITE CHOCOLATE & RASPBERRY CHEESECAKE

Serves: 12

Prep: 30 minutes
Set: 6+ hours
Lasts: 3+ days, in the fridge

BASE:
300g digestive biscuits
100g unsalted butter, melted

FILLING:
250g white chocolate
500g full-fat soft cheese
1 tsp vanilla extract
100g icing sugar
300ml double cream
250g raspberries

DECORATION (OPTIONAL):
75g white chocolate, melted
150ml double cream
2 tbsp icing sugar
12 raspberries
Grated white chocolate
5g freeze-dried raspberries

CUSTOMISE:
Fold 75ml raspberry coulis through the filling for an extra raspberry swirl.

You can also fold through 150g chopped white chocolate if you wanted some delicious chunks!

Swap the white chocolate for milk chocolate, dark chocolate, or even leave out completely.

White chocolate and raspberry is such a great combination for me and it seems my blog readers love it too! The raspberries swirl into the sweet cheesecake mix and create a wonderful pocket of sharpness. I like to go all-out with the decorations, but you can decorate this cheesecake however you like.

Blitz the biscuits to a fine crumb in a food processor, or bash with a rolling pin in a bowl. Mix the melted butter into the biscuits, then press the mixture into the base of a deep, 20cm springform cake tin and refrigerate while you make the filling.

Melt your white chocolate until smooth – I do this in the microwave, but you can also do it in a heatproof bowl set over a pan of simmering water (bain-marie). Leave the chocolate to cool for 5–10 minutes.

In a separate bowl, add the soft cheese, vanilla extract and icing sugar and whisk until smooth. Add the melted and cooled white chocolate and whisk again until smooth. Pour in the double cream and whisk again. (Alternatively, you can whip the cream separately to soft peaks, and then fold this through the cream cheese/chocolate mix.)

Once the mixture has been combined, fold through the raspberries; the mixture should swirl slightly and turn partially pink as you mix! Spread over the chilled biscuit base and then return to the fridge to set for at least 6 hours, or preferably overnight.

Once set, carefully remove the cheesecake from the tin. Drizzle over some melted white chocolate – you can use a teaspoon or a piping bag. Whip the cream and icing sugar together to soft peaks and pipe 12 swirls onto your cheesecake. Add a raspberry to the top of each swirl, then sprinkle over some grated chocolate and the freeze-dried raspberries.

NO-BAKE SALTED CARAMEL CHEESECAKE

Serves: 12

Prep: 30 minutes
Set: 6+ hours
Lasts: 3+ days, in the fridge

BASE:
250g digestive biscuits
75g salted pretzels
125g unsalted butter, melted

FILLING:
500g full-fat soft cheese
1 tsp vanilla extract
100g icing sugar
150g caramel sauce (I use shop-bought)
300ml double cream
1–2 tsp sea salt flakes

DECORATION (OPTIONAL):
75g caramel sauce
15–30g toffee popcorn
25g salted pretzels

CUSTOMISE:
If you want to keep this sweet, leave out the salt.

You can make your own caramel sauce if you want (see page 73), but I use shop-bought to make it easier.

If you want something even saltier, add extra sea salt. Sea salt is the best to add here as the flakes are delicious.

Sweet and salty is one of the most iconic combinations in the world. This winning cheesecake from my blog has a salty base, a sweet and salty filling, and even more on top with popcorn, pretzels and added caramel for decoration. I love popcorn, and my brother loves pretzels, so I wanted to incorporate them both for the best pudding ever and I am obsessed with the results. This cheesecake is HEAVEN.

Blitz the biscuits and pretzels to a fine crumb in a food processor, or bash with a rolling pin in a bowl. Pour in the melted butter and mix to combine. Press the mixture into the base of a deep, 20cm springform cake tin.

In a large bowl, add the soft cheese, vanilla extract, icing sugar and caramel sauce and whisk until smooth. Pour in the double cream and whisk again. (Alternatively, you can whip the cream separately to soft peaks, and then fold through the cream cheese mix.) Sprinkle in some salt a little at a time, tasting as you go so you know how much to add.

Once the mixture has thickened, spread it evenly over the biscuit base. Leave the cheesecake to set in the fridge for 5–6 hours, or preferably overnight.

Once set, remove from the tin. Drizzle some caramel sauce over the cheesecake and finish with some toffee popcorn and pretzels around the edge for decoration. Enjoy!

COOKIE DOUGH CHEESECAKE

Serves: 12

Prep: 1 hour
Bake: 5 minutes
Set: 6+ hours
Lasts: 3+ days, in the fridge

COOKIE DOUGH:
175g plain flour
125g unsalted butter, at room
    temperature
160g soft light brown sugar
½ tsp vanilla extract
Pinch of salt
30ml full-fat milk
125g dark or milk chocolate,
    finely chopped

BASE:
300g chocolate chip cookies
100g unsalted butter, melted

FILLING:
500g full-fat soft cheese
100g icing sugar
1 tsp vanilla extract
300ml double cream
Cookie dough balls (see recipe above)

DECORATION:
150ml double cream
2 tbsp icing sugar
Cookie dough balls (see recipe above)
Chocolate curls
Cookies

This recipe combines cookies and cheesecake and I adore it! The cheesecake still has a wonderful biscuit base to give it a bit of crunch, but the layer of cookie dough gives it a wonderful extra element. With cookie dough bites hidden inside the sweet vanilla cheesecake, and topped with even more, it's no surprise that this is one of the most requested bakes amongst my family and friends.

COOKIE DOUGH:
Preheat the oven to 200°C/180°C fan and line a baking tray with parchment paper. Sprinkle the plain flour onto the lined tray and bake for 5 minutes. Leave to cool fully.

Meanwhile, cream together the butter and sugar until the mixture is light and fluffy. Add the vanilla, toasted flour, salt, milk and chopped chocolate and beat again until smooth. Split the cookie dough into two halves. Set one half aside and portion the other half into small bite-sized balls, using a melon baller or two teaspoons. Chill in the fridge while you prepare the cheesecake base and filling.

BASE:
Blitz the cookies in a food processor to a fine crumb (or bash with a rolling pin in a bowl) and mix in the melted butter until combined. Tip the mixture into a deep, 20cm springform cake tin and press down firmly. Roll out the other half of the cookie dough you reserved earlier into a 20cm circle and put on top of the cookie base.

CUSTOMISE:

The biscuit base can be made with regular biscuits, or any other type of cookie.

You can make the filling chocolate-flavoured by adding 35g cocoa powder along with the icing sugar, or using 200g melted and cooled chocolate.

The chocolate chips for the cookie dough can be white, milk or dark chocolate, or a combination of all three.

You can use all of the cookie dough on top of the biscuit base, or you can use all of it folded through the cheesecake mix.

FILLING:

Using an electric mixer, mix the soft cheese, icing sugar and vanilla extract together until smooth. While whisking slowly, pour in the double cream and continue to whisk the mixture until it starts to thicken. (Alternatively, whip the cream separately to soft peaks and fold through the cream cheese mix.)

Once it has thickened, spread half of the cheesecake mixture onto the base and spread evenly. Add all but 6 of the cookie dough balls and cover with the rest of the cheesecake mixture. Cover and leave to set in the fridge for at least 6 hours, or preferably overnight.

DECORATION:

To decorate, whip together the double cream and icing sugar to soft peaks and use to pipe swirls onto the cheesecake. Top each swirl of cream alternately with the 6 cookie dough balls, or half a cookie. Sprinkle over chocolate curls and crushed cookies to finish.

NO-BAKE SPECULOOS CHEESECAKE

Serves: 12

Prep: 30 minutes
Set: 6+ hours
Lasts: 3+ days, in the fridge

BASE:
300g speculoos biscuits (I use Biscoff)
100g melted unsalted butter

FILLING:
500g full-fat soft cheese
1 tsp vanilla extract
100g icing sugar
250g speculoos biscuit spread
   (I use Biscoff)
300ml double cream

DECORATION (OPTIONAL):
75g speculoos biscuit spread, melted
150ml double cream
2 tbsp icing sugar
Speculoos biscuits

CUSTOMISE:
This recipe will work with any spread, such as chocolate or nut – just use the same amount as listed above.

The biscuits can be replaced with any other biscuit – yummy alternatives are gingernuts or digestives.

Okay, so I am a little obsessed with cheesecake (you might have noticed this if you have followed my blog for a few years). This one has always been so popular with my readers, and I have lost count of the amount of times I have made it. This spiced biscuit and spread give a wonderful, caramelised flavour to the base and cheesecake. Speculoos biscuit spread is SO good, and baking with it (or no-baking on this occasion) is the dreamiest of dreams.

Blitz the biscuits to a fine crumb in a food processor, or bash with a rolling pin in a bowl. Mix the melted butter into the biscuits, then press the mixture into the base of a deep, 20cm springform cake tin and refrigerate while you make the filling.

In a large bowl, add the soft cheese, vanilla extract and icing sugar and whisk until smooth. Add the biscuit spread and whisk again until smooth. Pour in the double cream and whisk again. (Alternatively, you can whip the cream separately to soft peaks, and then fold through the cheesecake mix.)

Once the mixture has thickened, spread the mixture over the biscuit base and leave the cheesecake to set in the fridge for at least 6 hours, or preferably overnight.

Once set, carefully remove the cheesecake from the tin. Drizzle over some melted biscuit spread – you can use a teaspoon or a piping bag. Whip the double cream and icing sugar together to soft peaks and then pipe onto your cheesecake in swirls. Add a biscuit to each swirl of cream, and then sprinkle over some crushed biscuit crumbs.

NO-BAKE PROSECCO CHEESECAKES

♥ Serves: 12

Prep: 30 minutes
Set: 4+ hours
Lasts: 3+ days, in the fridge

BASE:
150g digestive biscuits
60g unsalted butter, melted

FILLING:
150ml prosecco
12g (1 sachet) powdered gelatine
300g full-fat soft cheese
50g icing sugar (or caster sugar)
150ml double cream

DECORATION (OPTIONAL):
150ml double cream
2 tbsp icing sugar
12 strawberries
Edible gold dust

The perfect cheesecake for a celebration – individual Prosecco cheesecakes with a strawberry on top. I love a celebration and a party with friends and family. I am ALWAYS asked to bring dessert – and I really don't mind… I love it. However, when it's a special occasion, I love to bring out these Prosecco Cheesecakes!

Blitz the digestive biscuits to a fine crumb in a food processor, or bash with a rolling pin in a bowl. Mix the melted butter with the biscuits, then press the biscuits into the bases of a 12-hole loose-bottomed mini cake tin. Chill in the fridge while you make the filling.

Pour the prosecco into a small pan over a low heat, and heat until it's steaming and hot. Remove from the heat, pour in the gelatine and stir until the gelatine has dissolved fully. Leave to cool.

Add the soft cheese, vanilla extract and icing sugar to a bowl and whisk until smooth. Pour in the double cream, and whisk again until smooth. Finally, add the prosecco and mix until combined. Spread the mixture evenly between the 12 cheesecakes in the mini cake tin and place in the fridge to set for at least 4 hours, or overnight.

Once set, carefully remove the cheesecakes from the tin. To decorate your cheesecakes, whip the cream and icing sugar together and pipe onto your cheesecake in swirls. Add a strawberry to the top of each swirl of whipped cream, and sprinkle over some gold dust.

Image overleaf →

CUSTOMISE:

I use prosecco, but you can use champagne if you prefer!

You can make this in a deep, 20cm springform cake tin to create one large cheesecake.

The recipe can be halved to create 24 shot glass cheesecakes.

For an extra special prosecco flair, soak the strawberries in prosecco overnight before using to decorate the cheesecakes.

COCKTAIL HOUR:

You can also use other alcohols or classic cocktail combinations, as long as the amount of liquid still equals 150ml. For example:

- **G&T cheesecake**
  75ml gin + 75ml tonic water

- **Passion fruit martini cheesecake**
  50ml rum + 50ml passion fruit purée + 50ml prosecco

- **Strawberry daiquiri cheesecake**
  50ml rum + 100ml strawberry coulis

- **Espresso martini cheesecake**
  75ml vodka + 75ml strong espresso

NO-BAKE MALT CHOCOLATE CHEESECAKE

Serves: 12

Prep: 30 minutes
Set: 6+ hours
Lasts: 3+ days, in the fridge

BASE:
300g malted milk biscuits
100g unsalted butter, melted

FILLING:
150g milk chocolate
150g dark chocolate
500g full-fat soft cheese
75g icing sugar
100g malted drink powder
   (I use Horlicks)
1 tsp vanilla extract
300ml double cream

DECORATION (OPTIONAL):
150ml double cream
2 tbsp icing sugar
100g chocolate malt balls
   (I use Maltesers)

CUSTOMISE:
The cheesecake can be made with white, dark or milk chocolate – I just like the mix of milk and plain.

Other biscuits can be used for the base – or you can even mix in some chocolate malt balls. Use 200g biscuits and 150g chocolate malt balls mixed with the 100g melted butter.

When I think of a cosy drink, one that makes me feel all warm and fuzzy inside, I always think of something malt-related. When I was little I would have a warm malt drink on a cold wintery day, and it's now something that gives me great comfort. I love chocolate malt balls too, so combining these two beautiful things in a cheesecake is the perfect showstopper for any occasion and one that has found favour on my blog.

Blitz the biscuits to a fine crumb in a food processor, or bash with a rolling pin in a bowl. Mix the melted butter with the biscuits, then press the mixture into the base of a deep, 20cm springform cake tin and refrigerate while you make the filling.

Melt the milk and dark chocolate together in a heatproof bowl until smooth, either in the microwave or set over a pan of just simmering water (bain-marie). Leave the chocolate to cool for 5–10 minutes.

In a separate bowl, add the soft cheese, icing sugar, malted drink powder and vanilla extract and whisk until smooth. Add the melted and cooled chocolate and whisk again until smooth. Pour in the double cream and whisk again. (Alternatively, you can whip the cream separately to soft peaks, and then fold through the cream cheese/chocolate mix.)

Spread the mixture over the biscuit base and then return the cheesecake to the fridge to set for at least 6 hours, or preferably overnight.

Once set, carefully remove the cheesecake from the tin. Whip the cream and icing sugar together and pipe onto your cheesecake in swirls.

Add a chocolate malt ball to each whipped cream swirl, then sprinkle over some crushed chocolate malt balls too.

RED VELVET CHEESECAKE

♥ **Serves: 12**

Prep: 1 hour
Bake: 30–35 minutes
Set: 5–6+ hours
Lasts: 3+ days, in the fridge

RED VELVET CAKE:
75g unsalted butter
150g caster sugar
1 large egg
15g cocoa powder
1 tsp vanilla extract
1 tsp good-quality red food colouring
150ml buttermilk
150g plain flour
½ tsp bicarbonate of soda
1 tsp white wine vinegar

CHEESECAKE FILLING:
500g full-fat soft cheese
100g icing sugar
1 tsp vanilla extract
300ml double cream

DECORATION:
150ml double cream
2 tbsp icing sugar
Cake crumbs
Sprinkles (optional)

CUSTOMISE:
You can swap the classic red for other colours, but try and stick to a good-quality food colouring (I use Sugarflair).

The cheesecake can be flavoured with 200g melted chocolate.

When you bake a red velvet cake, you typically cover it in cream cheese frosting, so why not take that pairing one step further with a red velvet cake base and a delicious sweet vanilla cheesecake topping? You'll need a good-quality cake decorators' food colouring to get the deep red colour right. Just follow these simple steps for your new favourite dessert!

First make the cake. Preheat the oven to 170°C/150°C fan and line a 20cm cake tin with parchment paper.

Beat together the butter and caster sugar in a bowl until smooth. Add the egg and beat again until combined, then add the cocoa powder, vanilla extract and red food colouring and beat until the mixture is a lovely deep red colour.

Add the buttermilk and flour and beat briefly to combine before mixing in the bicarbonate of soda and white wine vinegar. Beat again for a couple of minutes until everything is smooth and incorporated well. Pour the mixture into the lined cake tin and bake for 30–35 minutes until a skewer poked into the middle of the cake comes out clean. Leave to cool in the tin for 10 minutes, then turn out onto a wire rack to cool fully. Once cooled, cut off a very small amount to use for the decoration later, and then return the cake to a clean 20cm cake tin lined with parchment paper.

Prepare the filling by whisking together the soft cheese, icing sugar and vanilla extract in a bowl until smooth. Pour in the double cream and whisk again. (Alternatively, you can whip the cream separately to soft peaks, and then fold through the cream cheese mix.) Once the mixture has thickened, spread it over the red velvet cake base, making sure to pack it into the sides of the tin. Leave the cheesecake to set in the fridge for 5–6 hours, or preferably overnight.

To decorate your cheesecake whip together the cream and icing sugar and pipe onto your cheesecake in swirls. Crumble over the small amount of cake that you cut off earlier and finish with some sprinkles if you like!

BAKED BROWNIE BOTTOM CHOCOLATE CHEESECAKE

Serves: 12

Prep: 30 minutes
Bake: 42–50 minutes
Set: 6+ hours
Lasts: 3+ days, in the fridge

BROWNIE BASE:
100g dark chocolate
100g unsalted butter
2 eggs
140g caster sugar
50g plain flour
25g cocoa powder

CHEESECAKE FILLING:
500g full-fat soft cheese
100g caster sugar
25g plain flour
2 eggs
1 tsp vanilla extract
100ml soured cream or crème fraîche
100g chocolate chips

DECORATION (OPTIONAL):
50g milk chocolate, melted
50g chocolate chips (any flavour)

A rich and soft baked brownie, topped with a deliciously creamy chocolate cheesecake. Typically brownies are made as a traybake, but why not make them into more of a dessert? With a thick and fudgy base and chocolate chip cheesecake topping this dessert is incredibly indulgent and makes a brilliant family bake.

First make the brownie base. Preheat the oven to 180°C/160°C fan and line the base of a deep, 20cm springform cake tin.

Melt the dark chocolate and butter together until smooth – you can do this in a microwave or in a bowl set over a pan of simmering water (bain-marie). Leave to cool for a few minutes.

In a separate bowl, whisk the eggs and caster sugar together for about 2–3 minutes. You want the mixture to double in volume and be light and fluffy. Add the melted chocolate mixture and fold through carefully, then add the flour and cocoa powder and fold through again. Pour the mixture into the lined tin and bake for about 12–15 minutes. You want there to be an ever-so-slight wobble in the middle once baked. Leave to cool in the tin. Increase the oven temperature to 220°C/200°C fan.

Whisk the soft cheese in a bowl to loosen it. Add the sugar and flour and whisk on a low speed until smooth. Whisk the eggs in a separate bowl, and then gradually add to the soft cheese, mixing again on a low speed. Add the vanilla extract. Fold through the soured cream or crème fraîche, then fold through the chocolate chips.

Pour the mix over the brownie base and smooth over in an even layer. Bake for 10 minutes, then reduce the temperature to 110°C/90°C fan and bake for a further 20–25 minutes. Once baked, turn off the oven and leave the cheesecake to cool in the oven with the door slightly ajar for 2 hours.

Once cooled, wrap the cheesecake in foil (still in the tin) and chill in the fridge overnight. Once chilled, run a knife around the edge of the tin, and carefully remove the cheesecake. Decorate by drizzling over some melted chocolate and sprinkling with some extra chocolate chips, if you like.

CUSTOMISE:

You can flavour this brownie really easily by adding in flavoured chocolate chips, or 1 tsp of flavouring such as orange, mint or coffee extract.

Add 150g chocolate chips to the brownie base before baking.

The cheesecake topping can be made chocolate flavoured by replacing the 25g plain flour with 50g cocoa powder.

BAKED LEMON & RASPBERRY CHEESECAKE

 Serves: 12

Prep: 30 minutes
Bake: 35–40 minutes
Cool: 2 hours
Lasts: 3+ days, in the fridge.

BISCUIT BASE:
300g digestive biscuits
100g melted unsalted butter

CHEESECAKE FILLING:
600g full-fat soft cheese
200g caster sugar
30g plain flour
Zest and juice of 2 lemons
3 eggs
175g soured cream or crème fraîche
250g raspberries (fresh or frozen)

DECORATION (OPTIONAL):
100g raspberries
15g freeze-dried raspberries
100ml raspberry coulis

When you combine lemon and raspberry together, you have a lovely contrast of sharp and sweet tangy flavours. So many different fruits can be used, but these are my favourites. I love a drizzle of raspberry coulis on top, with a few extra raspberries for good measure.

Preheat the oven to 220°C/200°C fan.

Blitz the biscuits to a fine crumb in a food processor, or bash with a rolling pin in a bowl. Pour in the melted butter and mix, then press into the base of a deep, 20cm springform cake tin. Put to the side while you make the filling.

In a bowl, whisk the soft cheese to loosen it. Add the sugar and flour, and whisk on a low speed until smooth, then add the lemon zest and juice and whisk briefly again.

Whisk the eggs in a separate bowl, then gradually pour into the cheesecake mix while mixing also on a low speed. Fold through the soured cream or crème fraîche, then add the raspberries. Pour the filling over the base in the tin and smooth over.

Bake for 10 minutes, then reduce the oven temperature to 110°C/90°C fan, and bake for a further 25–30 minutes. Once baked, turn off the oven and leave the cheesecake to cool in the oven with the door slightly ajar for 2 hours.

Wrap the cooled cheesecake in foil (still in the tin) and chill in the fridge overnight. Once chilled, run a knife around the edge of the tin, and carefully remove the cheesecake. Top with the fresh raspberries and freeze-dried raspberries and finish a drizzle of raspberry coulis, if you like.

CUSTOMISE:
The raspberries can be straight swapped for other fruits such as blueberries, blackberries, or even strawberries!

The lemon is optional if you just want a raspberry cheesecake, or the raspberries can be left out for a lemon cheesecake.

MAKE YOUR OWN RASPBERRY COULIS:
Simmer 100g fresh or frozen raspberries with 1 tablespoon of caster sugar in a pan until softened, then purée until smooth.

RHUBARB CRUMBLE CHEESECAKE

 Serves: 12

Prep: 30 minutes
Bake: 15–20 minutes
Set: 5–6+ hours
Lasts: 3+ days, in the fridge

CRUMBLE TOPPING:
120g plain flour
60g caster sugar
60g chilled unsalted butter, cubed

RHUBARB FILLING:
400g rhubarb, cut into 3cm pieces
75g caster sugar
½ tsp ground ginger (optional)
2 tbsp water

BASE:
300g digestive biscuits
100g unsalted butter, melted

CHEESECAKE FILLING:
500g full-fat soft cheese
100g icing sugar
1 tsp vanilla extract
150ml double cream

CUSTOMISE:
You can use any crumble-related fruit for this cheesecake, such as apples, apples and blackberries, plums or cherries. Just prepare the fruit in the same way.

The ginger can be replaced with another spice such as cinnamon, nutmeg, vanilla, or even orange zest.

Rhubarb and ginger together are a perfect combination; think rhubarb gin with ginger beer, rhubarb crumble with a hint of ginger in the crumble, yum. The beauty of this recipe is that it can be made with fresh rhubarb (when in season) or tinned. I love the creamy, soft centre of the cheesecake with crunchy crumble sprinkled all over the top.

CRUMBLE TOPPING:
Preheat the oven to 200°C/180°C fan. Put all the ingredients into a bowl and rub the mixture together with your fingers until it resembles breadcrumbs. Spread the mixture onto a tray, and bake for 15–20 minutes, mixing occasionally, or until it starts to brown. Leave the mixture on the tray to cool while you make the rhubarb filling.

RHUBARB FILLING:
Put the rhubarb into a heavy-based pan and sprinkle over the caster sugar, ground ginger and water. Cook the mixture over a medium heat for about 5–7 minutes while giving it a stir. You want the rhubarb to soften and hold some shape, without becoming mushy. Strain the mixture of any excess liquid and leave the mixture to cool fully while you make the base.

BASE:
Blitz the biscuits to a fine crumb in a food processor, or bash with a rolling pin in a bowl. Mix in the melted butter until combined and then press the mixture into the base of a deep, 20cm springform cake tin.

CHEESECAKE FILLING:
Put the soft cheese, icing sugar and vanilla into a bowl and whisk until smooth. Pour in the double cream and whisk again. (Alternatively, you can whip the cream separately to soft peaks, and then fold through the cream cheese mix.) Add the rhubarb mixture and fold together carefully.

Spread the mixture evenly over the biscuit base and then sprinkle over the baked crumble topping. Leave the cheesecake to set in the fridge for 5–6 hours, or preferably overnight.

Once set, carefully remove the cheesecake from the tin. Serve as it is, or with a drizzle of cream.

Cakes

When I think of baking, I think of cake. I think of a Victoria sponge, that absolute classic. How can so few ingredients (flour, sugar, butter, eggs) transform into the fluffy sponge of a cake? The chemistry behind baking will always fascinate me, and I will always enjoy eating it.

When filling and decorating cakes, there are so many options to go for, such as whipped cream, jam, fresh fruits, buttercreams and more! I love a classic sponge with a vanilla buttercream filling and jam – but I also love so many other variations too: carrot cake, sticky toffee cake, raspberry ripple… the endless number of flavours that you can work into a cake is incredible.

I had so much fun writing this chapter of the book; it was just the best getting to eat so many slices of cake. My friends and family were pretty happy too, as they got to test-run quite a few cakes!

A simple sponge (to serve 8–10) can be made by beating together:

- 250g unsalted butter
- 250g caster sugar
- 250g self-raising flour
- 5 medium eggs (which is roughly 250g, weighed in their shells)

MY TOP TIPS FOR CAKES:

1 Make sure you accurately measure your ingredients. Accuracy is so important as it will create the best texture and cake in the end – whether it's for a simple four-ingredient sponge, or a loaf cake.

2 Make sure your tin is the correct size and the oven is on the right setting – changing either of these can very heavily affect a cake, which we don't want!!

3 Use room temperature ingredients. I always keep my eggs at room temperature anyway, but if you keep them in the fridge, bring them back to room temperature before using. Baking spread can be used fridge cold, but unsalted butter is best at room temperature.

4 Try not to overmix your mixture. You want to mix just enough so that the ingredients are evenly and well distributed. Overmixing can knock too much air out of the cake mixture and result in a heavy texture.

5 Don't open your oven door too early. I know it's hard sometimes as you just want to see how your cake is baking, but opening the door can cause a cake to sink! Try and wait until the bake is at least three-quarters of the way through, and be quick!

GIN & TONIC LOAF CAKE

Serves: 8–10

Prep: 30 minutes
Bake: 45–50+ minutes
Cool: 2 hours
Lasts: 3+ days, at room temperature

250g unsalted butter
250g caster sugar
250g self-raising flour
5 eggs
Zest of 1 lime

G&T DRIZZLE:
75g caster sugar
5 tbsp gin
5 tbsp tonic water

DECORATION:
200g icing sugar
3–4 tbsp gin
Lime slices
Zest of 1 lime

CUSTOMISE:
Any flavour gin can be used!

The tonic water can be swapped for lemonade, ginger ale or more gin.

The lime is optional, or can be swapped for the zest of 1 orange or 1 lemon!

An absolutely iconic bake in the cake world is a lemon drizzle cake… and it got me thinking, why does the drizzle have to be lemon?! Why can't we add something else in, such as one of my favourite drinks – a G&T! And oh wow, it worked so much better than I ever thought it could – and my blog readers agree. The flavour from the drizzle works so well with the lime hinted sponge, and the gin icing topping just finishes it off to perfection!

Preheat the oven to 180°C/160°C fan and grease and line a 900g loaf tin.

Beat the butter and caster sugar together in a bowl until light and fluffy. Add the self-raising flour, eggs and lime zest to the bowl, and mix again until combined. Pour the mixture into the tin and for 45–50 minutes, or until baked through. Leave the cake to cool in the tin while you make the drizzle.

Add the caster sugar, gin and tonic water to a small pan and place over a low-medium heat. Stir gently until the sugar has dissolved and then turn off the heat.

Carefully poke holes into the top of the cake with a cake skewer or fork, then pour the drizzle over the cake. Leave the cake in the tin to cool fully.

Remove the cooled cake from the tin. Put the icing sugar into a bowl and gradually mix in the gin until you reach a thick and pourable consistency. Pour the icing over the cake, then finish with some lime slices and a sprinkling of lime zest.

CARROT LOAF CAKE

Serves: 8–10

Prep: 45 minutes
Bake: 50–60+ minutes
Cool: 2 hours
Lasts: 3+ days, in the fridge

175ml sunflower oil
3 large eggs
200g soft light brown sugar
250g grated carrots
100g raisins
Zest of 1 orange
200g self-raising flour
1 tsp bicarbonate of soda
2 tsp mixed spice
1 tsp ground ginger
1 tsp ground cinnamon
1 tsp grated nutmeg

CREAM CHEESE FROSTING:
125g unsalted butter, at room
    temperature
125g icing sugar
250g full-fat soft cheese
1 tsp vanilla extract

DECORATION:
Fondant carrots
Chopped nuts

CUSTOMISE:
The raisins can be swapped
for 100g walnuts, pecans, or a
combination of nuts and raisins.

Swap the cream cheese frosting
for a vanilla buttercream.

So... carrot cake. It's safe to say I am slightly obsessed with it, and it's a firm favourite on my blog too. My top flavour can change frequently but put a piece of carrot cake in front of me and I will always be happy. This spiced loaf cake topped with a cream cheese frosting is perfection in every bite – soft, moist and delicious. You basically can't go wrong with carrot cake. Honestly, it always works!

Preheat the oven to 180°C/160°C fan and grease and line a 900g loaf tin with parchment paper.

Put the sunflower oil, eggs and brown sugar into a large bowl and mix lightly until combined. Add the grated carrots, raisins and orange zest and fold through to combine, then add the self-raising flour, bicarbonate of soda and all the spices and mix again – take care not to overmix.

Pour the mixture into the tin and bake for 55–60 minutes. Sometimes it can take a little longer so test with a skewer – it should come out clean when inserted in the middle. Once baked, leave to cool in the tin for 10 minutes, then remove from the tin and leave to cool on a wire rack while you make the frosting.

Beat the butter in a bowl on its own for a few minutes to loosen it. Add the icing sugar, and beat again. I beat this for about 5 minutes to make it really smooth. Before you add the soft cheese, make sure it does not have any excess water; drain it away if it does. Add the soft cheese and vanilla extract and beat – it can go through a lumpy stage first, but eventually it will become smooth and thick!

Slather the cream cheese frosting over the cooled cake – I usually use an offset spatula. Decorate with fondant carrots and chopped nuts and enjoy!

COFFEE & WALNUT CAKE

❤ **Serves: 12+**

Prep: 30 minutes
Bake: 30–35+ minutes
Cool: 2 hours
Lasts: 3+ days, at room temperature

1 tbsp instant coffee granules
25ml boiling water
300g unsalted butter
300g soft light brown sugar
300g self-raising flour
6 eggs
100g chopped walnuts, plus extra
   to decorate

BUTTERCREAM:
1 tbsp instant coffee granules
25ml boiling water
200g unsalted butter
400g icing sugar

CUSTOMISE:
You can replace the fresh coffee with coffee extract, or even a shot of espresso from a coffee machine.

You can leave the walnuts out if you do not like them.

Use other nuts in place of the walnuts, such as pecans, macadamia nuts, pistachios or almonds.

Swap the soft light brown sugar for caster sugar or soft dark brown sugar.

Coffee cake with walnuts is such a classic combination – I love the taste of coffee cake, but oddly don't drink coffee that much – I'm more of a hot chocolate girl. However, a hot chocolate with a slice of coffee and walnut cake on the side is perfect. I love the light coffee-flavoured sponge, with the crunch of the walnuts in the sponge and on the top of the cake. The coffee-flavoured buttercream is smooth, silky and heavenly in every bite!

Preheat the oven to 180°C/160°C fan and grease and line two 20cm round cake tins with parchment paper.

Dissolve the coffee in the boiling water, and leave to cool.

Beat together the butter and soft light brown sugar until light and fluffy. Add the self-raising flour and eggs and beat again until combined. Pour the cooled coffee into the mix, and beat again, then fold through the chopped walnuts.

Split the cake mix evenly between the tins and bake the cakes for 30–35 minutes, or until a skewer inserted in the middle comes out clean. Let the cakes cool in the tins for about 10 minutes, then turn out onto a wire rack to cool fully while you make the buttercream.

Dissolve the coffee in the boiling water and leave to cool. Beat the butter on its own for about 5 minutes until nice and smooth. Add the icing sugar in two batches, beating in fully after each batch. Add the cooled coffee and mix again until smooth.

Place the first sponge on a plate and spread or pipe half of the buttercream over the top. Add the second layer and spread or pipe over the remaining buttercream. Finish by sprinkling over some chopped walnuts.

BLUEBERRY LIME LOAF CAKE

♡ Serves: 8–10

Prep: 30 minutes
Bake: 50–55+ minutes
Cool: 2 hours
Lasts: 3+ days, at room temperature

200g unsalted butter
200g caster sugar
200g self-raising flour, plus 1 tbsp
   for dusting
4 eggs
Zest of 1 lime
200g fresh or frozen blueberries

BUTTERCREAM:
125g unsalted butter, at room
   temperature
250g icing sugar
Juice of 1 lime

DECORATION:
100g blueberries
Lime zest

CUSTOMISE:

The blueberries can be swapped for any other berry you like, such as raspberries or blackberries.

The lime can also be switched for another citrus fruit, such as orange or lemon.

If you don't want to make a buttercream topping, make a lime drizzle instead by mixing 200g icing sugar with 3–4 tbsp lime juice.

When you bake with fruit, you often get beautiful colours dotted throughout the bakes. Combining berry and citrus flavours is always delicious too... lemon and raspberry, blackberry and lemon, or as in this cake, blueberry and lime. I adore it. Baking with blueberries always brings out their flavour and creates a delicious texture, and when topped with a simple buttercream frosting it's even better.

Preheat the oven to 180°C/160°C fan and grease and line a 900g loaf tin with parchment paper.

Put the butter and caster sugar into a bowl and beat until light and fluffy. Add the self-raising flour, eggs and lime zest to the bowl, and mix again until combined.

Put the tablespoon of plain flour into a bowl and add the blueberries, mixing until they are coated (this stops the blueberries all sinking to the bottom of the cake). Fold the blueberries through the cake mixture, then pour into the prepared tin and bake for 50–55 minutes, or until baked through. Remove the cake from the oven, and leave to cool fully in the tin while you make the buttercream.

Add the butter to a bowl and beat on its own for a few minutes to loosen and soften. Add the icing sugar and beat again until combined. Finally, add the lime juice and beat again.

Pipe or spread the buttercream onto the loaf cake, then sprinkle over the blueberries and lime zest.

VANILLA TRAYBAKE

💙 Serves: 12

Prep: 30 minutes
Bake: 45–50+ minutes
Decorate: 2 hours
Lasts: 3+ days, at room temperature

400g unsalted butter
400g caster sugar
8 eggs
400g self-raising flour
2 tsp vanilla extract

BUTTERCREAM:
250g unsalted butter, at room
    temperature
500g icing sugar
2 tsp vanilla extract
1–2 tbsp boiling water (optional)

DECORATION:
White chocolate 'jazzie' sweets
Fruit
Sprinkles

Traybake cakes are so much easier to serve at parties: you only need one tin, and you don't need to decorate them in any particularly fancy way. Bake the sponge, slather on some frosting, and you're done! This is a perfect easy bake for a bake sale or children's party.

Preheat the oven to 180°C/160°C fan and line a 23 x 33cm traybake tin with parchment paper.

In a bowl, mix the butter and caster sugar together until light and fluffy. Add the eggs, self-raising flour and vanilla extract to the bowl and beat again until combined. Pour the mixture into the lined tin and bake for 45–50 minutes, or until a skewer inserted in the middle comes out clean. Leave the cake to cool in the tin for 10 minutes, then turn out onto a wire rack to cool fully while you make the buttercream.

Add the butter to a bowl and beat on its own for a few minutes to loosen and soften it. Add the icing sugar and beat again until combined, then add the vanilla and beat again. If necessary, gradually add 1–2 tablespoons of boiling water, beating fully each time, to soften it slightly.

Spread the buttercream onto the cake and decorate the top with white chocolate 'jazzies', fruit, sprinkles – or whatever you want!

CUSTOMISE:
Make it a chocolate sponge by replacing 75g of the self-raising flour with 75g cocoa powder.

Make a chocolate buttercream by replacing 50g of the icing sugar with 50g cocoa powder.

The buttercream can be flavoured with caramel by adding 75g caramel sauce (see page 73).

STICKY TOFFEE CAKE

Serves: 12+

Prep: 45 minutes
Bake: 35–40+ minutes
Cool: 2 hours
Lasts: 3+ days, at room temperature

CAKE:
250g pitted dates (I use Medjool)
1½ tsp bicarbonate of soda
180ml boiling water
125g unsalted butter
225g soft dark brown sugar
4 eggs
250g self-raising flour
125g black treacle
1–2 tsp vanilla extract

SAUCE:
150ml double cream
1 tbsp black treacle
75g soft dark brown sugar
50g unsalted butter

BUTTERCREAM:
200g unsalted butter
400g icing sugar
85g sticky toffee sauce (see above)

DECORATION:
Sticky toffee sauce (see above)
Sprinkles
Fudge pieces

When you think of cake, something like a Victoria sponge or a carrot cake probably springs to mind… but would you think of a sticky toffee cake? It's rich, fudgy, mouth-watering and utterly scrumptious. Just like my sticky toffee puddings, I am always going to enjoy a cake like this. Make it as a two-layer cake like I have here, or even as cupcakes, a traybake or a loaf cake!

CAKE:

Preheat the oven to 180°C/160°C fan and line two 20cm round cake tins with parchment paper.

Chop the dates into quarters and add to a small bowl with the bicarbonate of soda and boiling water. Leave to sit for 10 minutes, then tip into a food processor or blender and blitz to a smooth purée.

Put the butter and soft dark brown sugar into a large bowl and beat until combined and smooth. Add the eggs to the bowl one at a time, beating after each one. Finally add the self-raising flour, black treacle, vanilla extract and puréed date mixture and beat again until smooth.

Pour the mixture evenly into the two tins and bake for 35–40 minutes, or until a skewer inserted in the middle comes out clean. Once baked, leave the cakes to cool for 10 minutes in the tins, then remove and leave to cool fully on a wire rack while you make the sauce.

SAUCE:

Put the double cream, black treacle, soft dark brown sugar and butter into a pan, and place over a low heat until the butter has melted and everything is combined. Bring the mixture to the boil and bubble for 1 minute, then remove from the heat and leave to cool fully. Stir occasionally so a skin does not form on the top of the sauce.

Continued overleaf →

BUTTERCREAM:
Beat the butter for 3–5 minutes until smooth, then add the icing sugar and beat again until it's fully mixed in. Add 85g of the sticky toffee sauce and beat again.

DECORATION:
Pipe or spread half of the buttercream onto the first sponge. Put the second sponge on top and then top with the rest of the buttercream. Drizzle some more sticky toffee sauce on to the cake (any leftover sauce can be served with the cake), and then sprinkle with your favourite sprinkles and some fudge pieces.

CUSTOMISE:
Swap the dark brown sugar for light brown sugar.

Use golden syrup instead of treacle for a lighter flavour.

The mixture can be poured into a 23 x 33cm traybake tin and baked for 50–60 minutes.

The mixture can be poured into a 900g loaf tin and baked for 50–60 minutes.

The mixture will make 24–26 cupcakes; bake for 20–22 minutes.

If you're short on time, use shop-bought toffee sauce.

COCONUT CAKE

♥ **Serves: 12+**

Prep: 30 minutes
Bake: 30–35+ minutes
Cool: 2 hours
Lasts: 3+ days, at room temperature

175g unsalted butter
250g caster sugar
300g self-raising flour
1 tsp baking powder
4 eggs
275ml tinned coconut milk
75g desiccated coconut

BUTTERCREAM:
200g unsalted butter, at room
    temperature
400g icing sugar
50–75ml coconut milk

DECORATION:
25g coconut flakes or
    desiccated coconut

CUSTOMISE:
Halve the mixture and use to make
12–14 cupcakes. Bake them for
20–22 minutes.

You can also make a three layer
cake; increase the cake ingredient
amounts by 50 per cent and bake
in three 20cm tins.

This cake is light, fresh and so very coconutty. It's slightly different to a basic cake of just butter, sugar, flour and eggs but the extra ingredients make all the difference. The coconut milk and desiccated coconut bring such a delicious flavour to the sponge and create the best texture. A creamy coconut buttercream frosting is slathered over the cake which is then topped with lightly toasted coconut... YUMMY.

Preheat the oven to 180°C/160°C fan and grease and line two 20cm round cake tins with parchment paper.

Beat the butter and caster sugar together until light and fluffy. Add the self-raising flour, baking powder and eggs and beat again until combined. Gradually add the coconut milk, slowly mixing all the time, until combined. Finally fold through the desiccated coconut.

Split the cake mix evenly between the two tins and bake the cakes for 30–35 minutes. Let the cakes cool in the tins for about 10 minutes, then turn out onto a wire rack to cool fully while you make the buttercream.

Beat the butter on its own for about 5 minutes until nice and smooth. Add the icing sugar in two batches, beating well after each addition. Gradually add the coconut milk until smooth and fluffy.

Place the first sponge on a plate and spread or pipe half of the buttercream onto the top. Add the second cake and spread or pipe over the remaining buttercream.

Toast the coconut flakes or desiccated coconut in a dry frying pan over a low-medium heat, moving the coconut about until it browns slightly. Sprinkle over the toasted coconut to finish!

DEATH BY CHOCOLATE CAKE

 Serves: 15+

Prep: 45 minutes
Bake: 30–35+ minutes
Cool: 2 hours
Lasts: 3+ days, at room temperature

275g dark chocolate
275g unsalted butter
1 tbsp instant coffee granules
125ml boiling water
250g plain flour
40g cocoa powder
1½ tsp baking powder
¼ tsp bicarbonate of soda
250g caster sugar
250g soft light brown sugar
5 eggs
100ml buttermilk

CHOCOLATE FROSTING:
250g unsalted butter, at room
  temperature
500g icing sugar
50g cocoa powder
1 tsp vanilla extract
75–125ml evaporated milk

DECORATION:
Chocolate chips or chocolate curls

When you think of chocolate cake, there are so many variations... so, why not take it to the next level and create a cake so chocolatey that you will never want to make another chocolate cake ever again? Three layers of chocolate fudge cake, the best chocolate frosting you will ever make, and even more chocolate perfection for the decoration. Hello heaven!

Preheat the oven to 160°C/140°C fan and grease and line three 20cm round cake tins with parchment paper.

Melt the dark chocolate and butter until combined. I do this in a microwave in 30-second bursts, but you can use a heatproof bowl set over a pan of just simmering water (bain-marie). Meanwhile, put the instant coffee granules into a cup and pour over the boiling water; stir until smooth. Add the coffee to the chocolate/butter mix and stir until smooth.

Put the flour, cocoa powder, baking powder, bicarbonate of soda, caster sugar and soft light brown sugar into a large bowl and mix well. Beat the eggs with the buttermilk in a separate bowl, then add to the dry ingredients and combine with the chocolate/butter mix, folding carefully and gently until smooth.

Pour the mixture evenly into the three tins and bake for 30–35 minutes. Once baked, leave to cool in the tins for 10 minutes, then transfer to a wire rack to cool fully while you make the chocolate frosting.

CUSTOMISE:

This recipe can be baked in two 20cm cake tins instead of three if you prefer – increase the baking time to 35–40 minutes.

The chocolate chips/curls on the outside of the cake are optional – decorate the top of the cake any way you like!

Chocolate-coated strawberries would be the ultimate topping for this cake if you wanted to take it to another new level.

Beat the butter on its own in a bowl for a few minutes to loosen it. Add the icing sugar and the cocoa powder in two batches, beating well after each addition. Add the vanilla extract and gradually pour in the evaporated milk, a little at a time, mixing well as you go. You want it to combine well so you do not want to add too much, too soon. The more evaporated milk you add the runnier it will be. I have found about 75–125ml is perfect for me but if the weather is a little warmer, you may find you need less.

Add the first sponge to a plate or serving board, and spread some of the frosting on top of the cake. Repeat with the second sponge, then add the third sponge on top and spread the remaining buttercream on the top and sides of the cake – it doesn't have to be neat! Carefully press chocolate chips or chocolate curls into the sides of the cake for an extra chocolate hit!

Image overleaf →

WHITE CHOCOLATE RASPBERRY CAKE

Serves: 12

Prep: 30 minutes
Bake: 40–45+ minutes
Decorate: 2 hours
Lasts: 3+ days, at room temperature

250g unsalted butter
250g caster sugar
5 eggs
250g self-raising flour
1 tsp baking powder
200g fresh raspberries

WHITE CHOCOLATE BUTTERCREAM:
200g white chocolate
200g unsalted butter, at room
   temperature
450g icing sugar
1–2 tbsp boiling water (optional)

DECORATION:
50g white chocolate, melted
100g fresh raspberries
5g freeze-dried raspberries

CUSTOMISE:
The white chocolate can
be swapped for milk or dark
chocolate... or flavoured chocolate!

The raspberries can be replaced
with strawberries, blueberries or
blackberries.

This recipe will make 24 cupcakes
– bake for 20–22 minutes.

I have always adored the combination of chocolate and berries. Raspberries and white chocolate is one of the more common pairings (strawberry and milk chocolate is another one) but you can customise this cake however you like. I wanted to create a cake that would be light, fruity, and still have the chocolatey sweetness that I always crave... this cake was the answer.

Preheat the oven to 180°C/160°C fan and line two 20cm round cake tins with parchment paper.

In a bowl, mix the butter and caster sugar together until light and fluffy. Add the eggs, self-raising flour and baking powder to the bowl and beat again until combined. Fold through the raspberries.

Split the mixture evenly between the two tins and bake for 40–45 minutes. Once baked, leave the cakes to cool in the tins for 10 minutes, and then turn out onto a wire rack to cool fully while you make the buttercream.

Melt the white chocolate in the microwave, or in a bowl set over a pan of simmering water (bain-marie) until smooth. Leave the chocolate to cool for 10 minutes.

Add the butter to a clean bowl and beat on its own for a few minutes to loosen and soften. Add the icing sugar and beat again until combined, followed by the melted and cooled white chocolate. If the mixture is a little stiff, add 1–2 tablespoons of boiling water as needed, beating fully each time, to soften it slightly.

Place the first sponge onto a serving plate, and pipe or spread half of the white chocolate buttercream frosting over the sponge. Add the second sponge, and pipe or spread the remaining buttercream on top. Decorate the top with a drizzle of melted white chocolate, fresh raspberries and a sprinkle of freeze-dried raspberries.

COOKIES & CREAM
DRIP CAKE

Serves: 15

Prep: 30 minutes
Bake: 25–30+ minutes
Decorate: 2 hours
Lasts: 3+ days, at room temperature

400g unsalted butter
400g soft light brown sugar
8 eggs
325g self-raising flour
75g cocoa powder
1 tsp baking powder

**COOKIES & CREAM
BUTTERCREAM:**

300g unsalted butter, at room
 temperature
650g icing sugar
150g cookies and cream biscuits
 (I use Oreos)
1–3 tbsp boiling water (optional)

DECORATION:
175g dark chocolate
½ tbsp sunflower or vegetable oil
12 cookies and cream biscuits,
 plus a few extra, crushed

Quite often, I get carried away when it comes to cake decoration... I love to go absolutely all out, and spend far too long on it, perfecting every single bit I can see (just take a look at my blog to see examples of this cake). The cookies and cream flavour in the buttercream frosting works SO unbelievably well with the chocolate sponges in this delicious drip cake.

Preheat the oven to 180°C/160°C fan and line three 20cm round cake tins with parchment paper.

In a bowl, mix the butter and soft light brown sugar together until light and fluffy. Add the eggs, self-raising flour, cocoa powder and baking powder and beat again until combined. Divide the mixture evenly between the three tins and bake for 25–30 minutes, or until baked through. Once baked, leave the cakes to cool in the tins for 10 minutes, then turn out onto a wire rack to cool fully while you make the buttercream.

Add the butter to a bowl and beat on its own for a few minutes to loosen and soften it. Add the icing sugar and beat again until combined.

Blitz the biscuits to a fine crumb in a blender or food processor and mix into the buttercream. If the mixture is very thick and hard to mix, gradually add 1–2 tablespoons of boiling water as needed to soften very slightly, mixing well each time.

Continued overleaf →

CUSTOMISE:
Make the sponges vanilla-flavoured – leave out the cocoa powder, increase the amount of self-raising flour to 400g and add 1 tsp vanilla extract.

The cookies and cream biscuits can be swapped for any other filled biscuits, such as custard creams, or bourbon biscuits.

You can use a ganache for the drip instead of the dark chocolate and oil: melt 75g dark chocolate and 75g milk chocolate and mix with 150ml double cream until smooth.

When you are ready to decorate, put the first cake onto a serving plate and evenly spread about 2 tablespoons of buttercream over the top. Add the second cake on top and repeat with the buttercream. Add the third and final cake to the top. Use a small amount of the buttercream to fill in any gaps around the sides and top and smooth over. Chill the cake for 15 minutes in the fridge. Once chilled, cover the top and sides of the cake with the remaining buttercream (reserve a little to make some buttercream swirls for the top of the cake later).

Melt the dark chocolate – I do this in the microwave but you can use a heatproof bowl set over a pan of just simmering water (bain-marie). Add the oil to the chocolate and stir until you reach a smooth dripping consistency.

Carefully pipe small amounts of the chocolate over the edge of the cake to create a drip. Once you have gone all around the cake, fill the top in with the rest of the chocolate, then return the cake to the fridge for 15 minutes to set the chocolate.

Decorate the cake by piping swirls of the reserved buttercream on the top. Add a biscuit to each swirl and then sprinkle over some crushed biscuits!

KEY LIME CAKE

❤ Serves: 12+

Prep: 30 minutes
Bake: 30–35+ minutes
Cool: 2 hours
Lasts: 3+ days, at room temperature

250ml sunflower or vegetable oil
4 eggs
325ml full-fat milk
Zest and juice of 2 limes
400g caster sugar
450g self-raising flour
1 tsp baking powder
½ tsp bicarbonate of soda

CREAM CHEESE FROSTING:
125g unsalted butter, at room
   temperature
125g icing sugar
250g full-fat soft cheese
Zest of 1 lime

DECORATION:
Lime slices

CUSTOMISE:

As key limes are extremely hard
to find in the UK, I recommend just
using regular limes. However, if
you can get hold of key limes, use
those for sure!

If you would rather a plain cream
cheese frosting, simply remove
the lime zest, or replace with 1 tsp
vanilla extract.

**This luscious and moist lime-flavoured sponge is topped
with a lime cream cheese frosting. It's indulgent without
being heavy… and I am obsessed with it. The use of oil
in the sponge makes a change from butter, and it works
incredibly well with the limes and milk creating the best
possible texture.**

Preheat the oven to 180°C/160°C fan and grease and line
three 20cm round cake tins with parchment paper.

Add the oil, eggs, milk, lime zest and juice to a large bowl
and whisk until smooth and combined, about 2 minutes.
Add the caster sugar, self-raising flour, baking powder and
bicarbonate of soda and fold through until combined.

Split the cake mix evenly between the three tins, and bake
for 30–35 minutes. Let the cakes cool in the tins for about
10 minutes, then turn out onto a wire rack to cool fully while
you make the cream cheese frosting.

Beat the butter in a bowl on its own for a few minutes to
loosen it. Add the icing sugar, and beat again. I beat this
for about 5 minutes to make it really smooth. Before you
add the soft cheese, drain it of any excess water, then add
to the bowl with the lime zest and beat thoroughly. It can
go through a lumpy stage first, but eventually the lumps
beat out and the mixture becomes smooth and thick.

Place the first sponge onto a plate and spread a third of
the cream cheese frosting on top.

Repeat with the other two sponges and remaining cream
cheese frosting. Finally, decorate with some slices of lime.

SALTED CARAMEL DRIP CAKE

Serves: 15

Prep: 30 minutes
Bake: 25–30+ minutes
Decorate: 2 hours
Lasts: 3+ days, at room temperature

400g unsalted butter
400g soft light brown sugar
8 eggs
400g self-raising flour
1 tsp baking powder

SALTED CARAMEL BUTTERCREAM:
300g unsalted butter, at room
　temperature
600g icing sugar
350g caramel sauce (I use Carnation)
Pinch of sea salt

DECORATION:
Chocolate caramel sweets
Sprinkles

CUSTOMISE:
Use caster sugar in the sponge for a lighter flavour, or soft dark brown sugar for a deeper caramel taste.

You can use a ganache for the drip instead of the caramel sauce: melt together 75g dark chocolate and 75g milk chocolate and mix with 150ml double cream.

Salted… caramel… drip… cake. Read those words, and tell me you don't want to bake it? If the reaction on my blog is anything to go by, this is one you'll love as well. Honestly, there are so many delicious things about this cake – just look at the oozy salted caramel sauce dripping down the sides!

Preheat the oven to 180°C/160°C fan and line three 20cm round cake tins with parchment paper.

In a bowl, mix the butter and soft light brown sugar together until light and fluffy. Add the eggs, self-raising flour and baking powder and beat again until combined. Pour the mixture evenly into the three tins and bake for 25–30 minutes, or until a skewer inserted in the middle comes out clean. Leave the cakes to cool in the tins for 10 minutes, then turn out onto a wire rack to cool fully while you make the buttercream.

Add the butter to a bowl and beat on its own for a few minutes to loosen and soften it. Add the icing sugar and beat again until combined.

Put the caramel sauce into a small bowl and add salt to taste – you don't want to spoil it by adding too much! When it's as you like it, add half the salted caramel sauce to the buttercream and beat until fully combined.

Put the first cake on a serving plate and evenly spread about 2 tablespoons of buttercream over the top. Add the second cake on top, and repeat with the buttercream. Finally, add the third and final sponge. Use a small amount of the buttercream to fill in any gaps on the sides and top and smooth over. Refrigerate the cake for 15 minutes. Once chilled, cover the top and sides of the cake with the remaining buttercream (reserve a little to pipe swirls on the cake later) and spread evenly.

Using a piping bag or spoon, carefully cover the top of the cake with the remaining caramel sauce and allow it to drip over the edges of the cake. You won't need much as the caramel sauce naturally falls quite far. Chill the cake in the fridge for 15 minutes to set help set the caramel.

Decorate the cake by using the reserved buttercream to pipe swirls on top of the cake. Finish with some chocolate caramel sweets and sprinkles.

Cupcakes
&
MUFFINS

Cupcakes are just mini cakes so have the same base ingredients... but there is something special about a lovely little cupcake.

When I was little, I made endless batches of fairy cakes or butterfly cupcakes. A cupcake is like having an individual portion of cake, but just taken to a whole new level – when topped with delicious icings and served in funky cupcake cases these cute little cakes become even more amazing. They are ideal for birthdays, parties, bake sales – you name it! Classic cupcake flavours are vanilla and chocolate but there are so many other flavours you can experiment with. In this book I have gone all out with some of my favourites: red velvet, cookie dough, brownie, and more! You'll also find delicious muffin recipes in this chapter too! Similar to cupcakes because they come in individual servings, muffins are a little larger in size and are usually un-iced; instead they have additional flavours baked into the muffin, whether chocolate chips, blueberries or banana chips. I love a muffin served with a cup of tea or a hot chocolate!

The main ingredients I use (to make 12 cupcakes) are:

- 150g unsalted butter
- 150g caster sugar
- 150g self-raising flour
- 3 medium eggs

Simply beat them together to create a thick and delicious cake batter and then pour into your cupcake cases. Other ingredients that crop up in regularly are cocoa powder, icing sugar and, of course, a variety of toppings!

MY TOP TIPS FOR CUPCAKES & MUFFINS:

1 Just like when baking a cake, you want all of the measurements and oven temperatures to be as accurate as possible for the best results.

2 Don't over-fill your cases. Paper case sizes can vary greatly, so only fill about two-thirds full, so that the mixture has enough room to rise and not overflow! Sometimes this can mean you get a few extra cupcakes out of a mix... but is that really a bad thing?!

3 Especially when using a new recipe, try to bake your cupcakes or muffins on the middle shelf of your oven. Some ovens will have hot spots, and areas that are too cold, so the centre is generally the best.

4 Allow your cupcakes or muffins to cool completely before decorating – just like most bakes, if something is too hot before you add anything on top, it will be a delicious mess!

PIÑA COLADA CUPCAKES

Makes: 12

Prep: 30 minutes
Bake: 20–25 minutes
Cool: 1 hour
Lasts: 2–3 days, at room temperature

150g unsalted butter or baking spread
150g caster sugar
3 eggs
150g self-raising flour
50g desiccated coconut
150g tinned pineapple, drained and
    cut into small chunks
50ml white rum (optional)

RUM BUTTERCREAM:
150g unsalted butter, at room
    temperature
300g icing sugar
2–3 tbsp white rum

DECORATION (OPTIONAL):
25g desiccated coconut
75g pineapple, in small chunks
Mini straws/party decorations

Think of a cocktail in cupcake form and you have these beauties. Coconut, pineapple and rum, all in a cake. I am biased, obviously, but I absolutely adore these cupcakes. The desiccated coconut gives them a lovely flavour, and the chunks of pineapple throughout have a yummy texture. The topping is sweet, but deliciously hinted with rum. A perfect cupcake!

Preheat the oven to 180°C/160°C fan and get 12 cupcake cases ready.

Beat the butter with the caster sugar until light and fluffy. Add the eggs, self-raising flour and desiccated coconut and mix until combined. Add the pineapple and rum, if using, and fold through until combined.

Spoon the mix evenly into the cupcake cases and bake for 20–25 minutes until they are baked through and springy to touch. Leave to cool on a wire rack while you make the buttercream.

Beat the butter until smooth – this can take a couple of minutes. Add the icing sugar in two batches, beating well after each addition. Finally add the white rum and beat again until smooth.

Pipe or spread the buttercream onto your cupcakes. Sprinkle over some desiccated coconut and add some small chunks of pineapple. Finish with a mini straw, or party decoration!

CUSTOMISE:
The rum is optional – it can be replaced with creamed coconut for an alcohol-free cupcake.

For a stronger coconut flavour, lightly toast the desiccated coconut in a dry frying pan for a few minutes over a low heat.

You can add a rum drizzle to the cupcake by heating 50ml white rum in a small pan with 75g caster sugar and spooning over the cupcakes just as they have come out of the oven.

WHITE CHOCOLATE & PISTACHIO CUPCAKES

 Makes: 12

Prep: 45 minutes
Bake: 18–22 minutes
Cool: 1 hour
Lasts: 3+ days, at room temperature

150g unsalted butter or baking spread
150g caster sugar
3 eggs
150g self-raising flour
150g white chocolate chips
150g pistachios, chopped

WHITE CHOCOLATE BUTTERCREAM:
125g unsalted butter, at room temperature
250g icing sugar
150g white chocolate, melted and cooled

DECORATION:
75g white chocolate, melted
50g pistachios, chopped

Just like white chocolate and raspberry, I adore the combination of white chocolate and pistachio. Pistachio nuts have such an iconic flavour and they marry so well with the sweetness of white chocolate. You can, of course, use a different chocolate if you prefer, but honestly... these are the best.

Preheat the oven to 180°C/160°C fan and get 12 cupcake cases ready.

Cream together the butter and caster sugar until light, fluffy and smooth. Add the eggs and self-raising flour and beat again until smooth. Fold through the chocolate chips and chopped pistachios.

Spoon the mix evenly into the cupcake cases and bake for 18–22 minutes, or until cooked through. Leave to cool on a wire rack while you make the buttercream.

Beat the butter until smooth. Add the icing sugar and mix until combined, then beat for at least 2 minutes. Pour in the melted white chocolate and mix again until smooth.

Pipe or spread the buttercream onto the cupcakes, then drizzle over the melted white chocolate and sprinkle with chopped pistachios.

CUSTOMISE:
I use plain unshelled pistachios when baking, but if you like salted ones there's nothing to stop you using them for the decoration.

The white chocolate can be swapped for milk or dark chocolate.

If you would rather a plain sponge, you can leave out the chocolate chips and pistachios, or just use one or the other.

If you don't like pistachios, other nuts such as walnuts, pecans or macadamias work really well too.

HONEYCOMB CUPCAKES

Makes: 12

Prep: 30 minutes
Bake: 18–22 minutes
Cool: 1 hour
Lasts: 2–3 days, at room temperature

150g unsalted butter or baking
   spread
150g soft light brown sugar
3 eggs
125g self-raising flour
25g cocoa powder

HONEY BUTTERCREAM:
150g unsalted butter, at room
   temperature
300g icing sugar
75g clear honey

DECORATION (OPTIONAL):
Chocolate-covered honeycomb bars
   (I use Crunchie)

When baking, you can experiment with all sorts of different flavours and additions to create what you like... but adding honey to buttercream? Well, my blog readers love this cupcake, so the answer is yes! I adore the combination of a chocolatey and light cupcake with a sweet but scrummy honey buttercream frosting – along with the honeycomb on top of course.

Preheat the oven to 180°C/160°C fan and get 12 cupcake cases ready.

Beat the butter with the soft light brown sugar until light and fluffy. Add the eggs, self-raising flour and cocoa and mix until combined. Spoon the mix evenly into the cupcake cases and bake for 18–22 minutes until they are baked through and springy to touch. Leave to cool on a wire rack while you make the buttercream.

Beat the butter until smooth – this can take a couple of minutes. Add the icing sugar, in two batches, beating well after each addition. Once all the sugar has been combined, add the honey and beat again until smooth. Pipe or spread the buttercream onto your cooled cupcakes, then add a piece of chocolate-covered honeycomb to each cupcake.

Image overleaf →

CUSTOMISE:

If you don't like honey, caramel sauce is a good alternative.

The cupcake sponge can be flavoured with vanilla: replace the cocoa powder with the same amount of self-raising flour and add 1 tsp vanilla extract.

You can make the cupcakes extra chocolatey by adding 100g chocolate chips (any flavour).

LEMON DRIZZLE CUPCAKES

Makes: 12

Prep: 30 minutes
Bake: 18–22 minutes
Cool: 1 hour
Lasts: 2–3 days, at room temperature

CUPCAKES:
150g unsalted butter or baking spread
150g caster sugar
3 eggs
150g self-raising flour
Zest of 1 lemon

DRIZZLE:
Juice of 2 lemons
75g caster sugar

LEMON BUTTERCREAM:
150g unsalted butter, at room
   temperature
300g icing sugar
Juice of ½ lemon

DECORATION (OPTIONAL):
Sprinkles
Lemon zest

CUSTOMISE:
These cupcakes can be made into
a DELICIOUS lemon drizzle cake –
just bake in a 20cm round cake tin
for 30–35 minutes.

You can mix the flavours up: use
lemon and lime, orange and
lemon, or a complete mixture!

Add a little texture by adding 1 tbsp
poppy seeds to the cake mixture.

Sometimes, going simple and classic is the way to success.
In this case, it's all things lemon because it is DELICIOUS.
To be fair, these lemon drizzle cupcakes have been one of
the most loved bakes on my blog in a long time. Anything
drizzled is always a hit, because it makes the cakes
themselves so tasty.

CUPCAKES:
Preheat the oven to 180°C/160°C fan and get 12 cupcake
cases ready. Beat the butter with the caster sugar until
light and fluffy. Add the eggs, self-raising flour and lemon
zest and mix until combined. Spoon the mix evenly into the
cupcake cases and bake for 18–22 minutes until they are
baked through and springy to touch.

DRIZZLE:
Mix together the lemon juice and caster sugar for the drizzle
in a bowl. Once the cupcakes are out of the oven, carefully
spoon the drizzle over the cupcakes, then leave them to
cool fully on a wire rack while you make the buttercream.

LEMON BUTTERCREAM:
Beat the butter until smooth – this can take a couple of
minutes. Add the icing sugar in two batches, beating well
after each addition, then add the lemon juice and beat again.

DECORATION:
Pipe or spread the buttercream onto your cupcakes, then
sprinkle each one with some sprinkles and lemon zest.

SALTED CARAMEL & CHOCOLATE CUPCAKES

 Makes: 12

Prep: 30 minutes
Bake: 18–22+ minutes
Cool: 1 hour
Lasts: 3+ days, at room temperature

CUPCAKES:
150g unsalted butter or baking spread
150g soft light brown sugar
3 eggs
125g self-raising flour
25g cocoa powder

SALTED CARAMEL SAUCE:
250g ready-made caramel
½ tsp sea salt

SALTED CARAMEL BUTTERCREAM:
125g unsalted butter, at room temperature
250g icing sugar
125g salted caramel sauce (see above)

DECORATION:
Salted caramel sauce
Grated chocolate
Sprinkles

CUSTOMISE:

If you don't like salted caramel, you can leave out the salt.

You can make the buttercream a salted caramel chocolate buttercream by replacing 25g of the icing sugar with 25g cocoa powder.

I love chocolate. And I love salted caramel. This cupcake has them combined in one bite. The sponges are light and the hidden salted caramel centre is smooth and always a nice surprise, while also topped with salted caramel buttercream frosting. Can you get anything any more delicious?!

CUPCAKES:
Preheat the oven to 180°C/160°C fan and get 12 cupcake cases ready. Cream together the butter and soft light brown sugar until light, fluffy and smooth. Add the eggs, self-raising flour and cocoa powder and beat again until smooth. Spoon the mix evenly into the cupcake cases and bake for 18–22 minutes, or until cooked through. Leave to cool on a wire rack while you make the salted caramel sauce.

SALTED CARAMEL SAUCE:
Mix the ready-made caramel with some sea salt – add the salt gradually and taste as you go! (Alternatively, you can use a ready-made salted caramel sauce.) Core out a small amount of cake from each cupcake and add a heaped teaspoon of salted caramel per cupcake.

SALTED CARAMEL BUTTERCREAM:
Beat the butter until smooth – this can take a couple of minutes. Add the icing sugar in two batches, making sure the sugar is fully incorporated each time. Once all of the sugar is in the mix and it's smooth, add the salted caramel (set a little aside to drizzle over your cupcakes) and beat until smooth.

DECORATION:
Pipe the buttercream onto the cupcakes, then drizzle over the leftover caramel sauce. Add some sprinkles and some grated chocolate if you fancy!

MAKE YOUR OWN CARAMEL:

- Put 250g white granulated sugar and 75ml water in a large pan and place over a low heat until the water has dissolved.

- Increase the heat and, without stirring, wait for the mixture to boil to an amber colour (this can take 5–10 minutes).

- Take the mixture off the heat, and pour in 200ml double cream, whisking like crazy to combine.

- Add 60g unsalted butter and whisk again. Finally, add 1 tsp vanilla extract and ½ tsp sea salt and whisk until smooth. Leave to cool completely.

COOKIE DOUGH CUPCAKES

Prep: 1 hour
Bake: 20–24 minutes
Cool: 1 hour
Lasts: 3+ days, at room temperature

COOKIE DOUGH:

65g unsalted butter or baking spread

65g soft light brown sugar

125g plain flour

Pinch of salt

25ml full-fat milk

½ tsp vanilla extract

100g dark or milk chocolate, finely chopped

CUPCAKES:

150g unsalted butter or baking spread

150g soft light brown sugar

3 eggs

150g self-raising flour

DECORATION:

150g unsalted butter, at room temperature

25g soft light brown sugar

275g icing sugar

1 tsp vanilla extract

12 mini cookies, plus a few crushed cookies

When you realise how much I adore cookies, and how much I love cupcakes, you will understand why this recipe is here. Combining different bakes is one of my favourite things to do – and when it's these two? HEAVEN! A cupcake stuffed with cookie dough and topped with buttercream flavoured with a brown sugar cookie dough... what more could you ask for?

First make the cookie dough. Add the butter and soft light brown sugar to a bowl and beat until smooth. Add the plain flour and salt and beat again. Add the milk, vanilla and chocolate and mix until combined.

Divide the dough into 12 pieces and roll into balls, then freeze for 30 minutes while you make the cupcakes

Preheat the oven to 180°C/160°C fan and get 12 cupcake cases ready. Beat the butter with the soft light brown sugar until the mixture is light and fluffy. Add the eggs and self-raising flour and mix until combined.

CUSTOMISE:

You can use all icing sugar in the buttercream instead of the light brown sugar and icing sugar.

You can make the cookie dough chocolate flavoured by replacing 25g of the plain flour with cocoa powder.

You can do the same for the cupcake mixture – replace 25g of the self-raising flour with 25g cocoa powder!

You can also top the cupcakes with small homemade cookies – I just love using shop-bought ones as they're crunchy.

Pop a frozen cookie dough ball into the bottom of each cupcake case, then spoon the mix evenly into the cupcake cases and bake for 20–24 minutes until they are springy to touch. Once baked, leave to cool on a wire rack while you make the buttercream.

Add the butter to a bowl and beat for about 3–4 minutes on its own to loosen it. Add the soft light brown sugar, icing sugar and vanilla and beat again for about 5 minutes. Pipe or spread the buttercream onto the cupcakes, then add a cookie per cupcake. Finish by sprinkling over some crushed cookie crumbs.

RED VELVET CUPCAKES

Makes: 12

Prep: 30 minutes
Bake: 20–25 minutes
Cool: 1 hour
Lasts: 2–3 days, in the fridge

75g unsalted butter or baking spread
150g caster sugar
2 eggs
1 tsp good-quality red food colouring
   (I use Sugarflair)
15g cocoa powder
1 tsp vanilla extract
125ml buttermilk
175g plain flour
1 tsp baking powder
½ tsp bicarbonate of soda
1 tsp white wine vinegar

CREAM CHEESE FROSTING:
150g unsalted butter, at room
   temperature
150g icing sugar
300g full-fat soft cheese
1 tsp vanilla extract

CUSTOMISE:
You can make your own buttermilk by whisking 1 tsp lemon juice into 125ml full-fat milk.

I always use a white wine vinegar for my red velvet cupcakes, but others can work such as apple cider vinegar.

Red velvet is one of those controversial cakes... why on earth does a cake need to have vinegar in it? Do I really have to use buttermilk?! You can of course just bake vanilla cupcakes and use food colouring, but red velvet is meant to be chocolate AND vanilla but still be super-red – the bicarbonate of soda, vinegar and buttermilk help create the texture and bring the colour out more. This cupcake recipe is one that my blog readers love and I'm sure you will too!

Preheat the oven to 180°C/160°C fan and get 12 cupcake cases ready. Beat together the butter and caster sugar in a stand mixer until smooth and fluffy. Add the eggs and beat again, then add the red food colouring, cocoa powder and vanilla extract and beat again – the colour should become a deep red.

Add the buttermilk and plain flour, and beat again, just until combined. Finally beat in the bicarbonate of soda, baking powder and white wine vinegar.

Spoon the mixture evenly between the 12 cases (make sure you only fill them two-thirds full) and bake for 20–25 minutes, or until a skewer inserted in the middle of the cupcakes comes out clean. Once baked, leave to cool on a wire rack while you make the frosting.

Beat the butter and icing sugar together until light and fluffy, just like a normal buttercream. I beat them together for about 5 minutes. Add the soft cheese and beat for about a minute, then scrape the sides of the bowl, and add the vanilla extract. Beat again for another minute, scraping down the sides of the bowl as needed. It should be a thick and smooth frosting once finished.

If you want to use some cake crumbs to decorate, level off any peaked cupcakes, or core a couple out slightly and crumble up.

Using a piping bag and a piping tip (I use a medium 2D closed star), pipe your cream cheese frosting onto the cupcakes. Finish by sprinkling over the cake crumbs.

PEANUT BUTTER & JELLY CUPCAKES

♡ Makes: 12

Prep: 45 minutes
Bake: 18–22+ minutes
Cool: 1 hour
Lasts: 3+ days, at room temperature

Peanut butter and jelly is a classic flavour combo, usually found in America. We call jelly jam over here, but peanut butter and jelly has such a good ring to it! These peanut butter flavoured cupcakes are so tasty – filled with a sweet raspberry jam and topped with a creamy peanut butter frosting, you can't really go wrong!

CUPCAKES:

150g unsalted butter or baking spread
150g caster sugar
3 eggs
150g self-raising flour
100g smooth peanut butter
75ml full-fat milk

PEANUT BUTTER BUTTERCREAM:

125g unsalted butter, at room
    temperature
250g icing sugar
100g smooth peanut butter
2–3 tbsp full-fat milk

FILLING:

200g raspberry jam

DECORATION:

50g salted peanuts, chopped
50g raspberries

CUSTOMISE:

I used raspberry jam but you can use any flavour jam you like.

I used smooth peanut butter to make it easier to blend for the buttercream, but you can use crunchy in the cupcakes if you prefer.

CUPCAKES:

Preheat the oven to 180°C/160°C fan and get 12 cupcake cases ready. Cream together the butter and caster sugar until light, fluffy and smooth. Add the eggs, self-raising flour, peanut butter and milk and beat again until smooth. Spoon the mix evenly into the cupcake cases and bake for 18–22 minutes, or until cooked through. Leave to cool on a wire rack while you make the buttercream.

PEANUT BUTTER BUTTERCREAM:

Beat the butter until smooth. Add the icing sugar in two batches, beating well after each addition until smooth. Beat this mixture for at least 2 minutes, then add the peanut butter and mix again until smooth. Add the milk, a tablespoon at a time, until you reach your desired consistency.

FILLING AND DECORATION:

Core out the middle of each cooled cupcake and spoon in the jam. You can either press the sponge circles back on the cupcakes – or just snack on them! Pipe or spread the buttercream onto the cupcakes, then sprinkle over some chopped peanuts, and add some fresh raspberries.

BROWNIE CUPCAKES

♥ **Makes: 12**

Prep: 15 minutes
Bake: 20–22 minutes
Cool: 1 hour
Lasts: 2–3 days, at room temperature

100g unsalted butter or baking spread
100g dark chocolate
2 eggs
150g soft light brown sugar
50g plain flour
25g cocoa powder
75g dark chocolate chips
75g milk chocolate chips

FROSTING:
125g unsalted butter, at room
  temperature
250g icing sugar
25g cocoa powder
50ml evaporated milk or double cream

DECORATION:
50g chocolate chips or chocolate curls

CUSTOMISE:
The chocolate chips you use in the cupcakes can be any flavour you like – I just love using a mixture of milk and dark chocolate.

The cupcakes are perfect without the topping as well if you want a small brownie!

Think fudgy, think chocolatey, think one of the most indulgent cupcakes you will ever bake and you get these bad boys. They are the combination of all delicious things... even if you don't like chocolate I am confident that these will change your mind. The cupcakes themselves are made up of a lovely fudge brownie mixture, topped with a luscious chocolate frosting and even more chocolate on top. YUM.

Preheat the oven to 180°C/160°C fan and get 12 cupcake cases ready.

Melt together the butter and dark chocolate in a heatproof bowl set over a pan of just simmering water, or in the microwave for 1–2 minutes. Leave to cool to room temperature.

Using an electric whisk/stand mixer, whisk together the eggs and soft light brown sugar for a few minutes until the colour has turned pale and the mixture leaves a trail for a couple of seconds. Pour the cooled chocolate over the eggs and fold together carefully. Once combined, tip the plain flour and cocoa powder into the bowl and then gently fold together. Finally, fold through the chocolate chips.

Spoon the mixture evenly into the cupcake cases and bake for 20–22 minutes until they are baked through and springy to touch. Leave to cool on a wire rack while you make the frosting.

In a bowl, beat the butter on its own for a few minutes to loosen it. Add the icing sugar and cocoa powder in two batches, beating well after each addition. Pour in the evaporated milk or double cream, a little at a time, mixing as you go until fully combined.

Once the cupcakes have cooled, pipe or spread the frosting onto the cupcakes. Top with some more chocolate chips or chocolate curls for decoration.

BANOFFEE CUPCAKES

♥ Makes: 12

Prep: 30 minutes
Bake: 18–22 minutes
Cool: 1 hour
Lasts: 2–3 days, in the fridge

150g unsalted butter or baking spread
150g soft light brown sugar
2 eggs, beaten
2 overripe medium bananas, mashed
175g self-raising flour

DECORATION:
150g caramel sauce
300ml double cream
2 tbsp icing sugar
1 tsp vanilla extract
Chocolate shavings
Dried banana chips or 1 banana,
    chopped

An amazing thing about baking with bananas is that you can use up the bananas that you forgot about – the ones that have become slightly brown and squishy are perfect for cake. This sponge is made with soft light brown sugar and mashed banana, stuffed with a caramel sauce, topped with sweetened whipped cream and finished with chocolate shavings. It's basically banoffee pie in cupcake form!

Preheat the oven to 180°C/160°C fan and get 12 cupcake cases ready.

Beat the butter with the soft light brown sugar until light and fluffy. Add the eggs, mashed bananas and self-raising flour and mix until combined.

Spoon the mix evenly into the cupcake cases and bake for 18–22 minutes until they are baked through and springy to touch. Leave to cool on a wire rack.

When you are ready to decorate, core out a small amount of the sponge, and fill each hole with 1 heaped teaspoon of caramel. Whip the cream with the icing sugar and vanilla extract to soft peaks and then pipe onto your cupcakes in swirls. Decorate with some more caramel sauce, chocolate shavings and either some dried banana chips or fresh banana pieces.

CUSTOMISE:
You can use a vanilla buttercream to top the cupcakes if you do not like fresh cream. Use 150g room temperature unsalted butter, 300g icing sugar, and 1 tsp vanilla extract.

If you don't want to use banana in the sponge, leave out the mashed banana and use 3 eggs instead of 2.

Add 100g chocolate chips to the sponge to create a chocolate chip banana cupcake.

Make the cake chocolate flavoured by replacing 25g of the self-raising flour with 25g cocoa powder.

TRIPLE CHOCOLATE MUFFINS

Makes: 9–10

Prep: 15 minutes
Bake: 25 minutes
Cool: 1 hour
Lasts: 2–3 days, at room temperature

115g unsalted butter or baking spread
250g caster sugar
2 eggs
225g self-raising flour
25g cocoa powder
Pinch of salt
125ml full-fat milk
75g dark chocolate chips
75g milk chocolate chips
75g white chocolate chips

Sometimes in life, you just need a whole lot of chocolate. These triple chocolate muffins are the answer to everything, especially as they are so incredibly easy to bake. I'm utterly in love with this recipe and it's a firm favourite on the blog too. Eating one of these warm out of the oven is just the best thing ever, and I wholeheartedly recommend you try it!

Preheat the oven to 190°C/170°C fan and get your muffin cases ready – I like to use tulip-style muffin cases.

Beat the butter with the caster sugar until light and fluffy. Add the eggs one at a time, beating well after each addition.

Add the self-raising flour, cocoa powder and salt to the mixture, and beat again. Finally, pour in the milk and beat again until just combined – try not to over-beat the mixture!

Fold through all the chocolate chips, and spoon the mixture evenly into the muffin cases. Bake for about 25 minutes, or until they are baked through and springy to touch.

MAKE A SOFT CENTRE:

- Freeze 25g spoonfuls of chocolate spread for 1 hour.

- Half-fill the muffin cases with the mixture, then add a frozen chocolate spread ball.

- Cover with the remaining mixture before baking as above.

CUSTOMISE:

The chocolate chips you use in the muffins can be any flavour you like – I just love using three different flavours for a delicious muffin.

The chocolate chips can be swapped to chunks of chocolate if you prefer bigger pieces.

If you want an orange- or mint-flavoured chocolate muffin you can easily add 1 tsp orange or peppermint extract when you add the eggs.

BANANA, CHOCOLATE & HAZELNUT MUFFINS

♥ Makes: 12

Prep: 15 minutes
Bake: 25 minutes
Cool: 1 hour
Lasts: 2–3 days, at room temperature

3 overripe medium bananas, mashed
200g soft light brown sugar
2 eggs
50ml sunflower or vegetable oil
1 tsp vanilla extract
275g self-raising flour
Pinch of salt
200g chocolate hazelnut spread

Baking with overripe bananas is the best – it means they don't go to waste, and you get something delicious out of it. The bananas create a yummy flavour, as well as making part of the best muffin batter – so when you mix this with a bit of chocolate hazelnut spread, you have a winner. These muffins are always a hit, whether it's for breakfast, a dessert or just because you fancy something sweet!

Preheat the oven to 190°C/170°C fan and get your muffin cases ready – I like to use tulip-style muffin cases.

Put the mashed bananas, soft light brown sugar, eggs, oil and vanilla extract into a large bowl and whisk until smooth. Add the self-raising flour and salt and mix again until just combined – make sure you don't overmix. Spoon the mixture evenly into the muffin cases; they should be about three-quarters full.

Melt the chocolate hazelnut spread slightly in the microwave until smooth and add a teaspoonful to each muffin. Use a skewer to swirl this in slightly. Bake for about 25 minutes, or until they are baked through and springy to touch.

CUSTOMISE:

If you want these muffins to be extra chocolatey, you can add up to 175g chocolate chips into the mix, after you add the self-raising flour and salt.

The chocolate hazelnut spread can be left out if you just want banana muffins – or you can spread some more on top after baking if you want an extra chocolate hazelnut boost!

Use caster sugar instead of the soft light brown sugar if you want a lighter flavour.

Cookies are probably one of my favourite things to bake...
I always think that cookie dough is one of the best things to
make when you are in a baking mood but don't want to have
a lot to think about, and they are so simple to customise.
Easy to bake, and even easier to eat.

I nearly always make my cookie dough with a stand mixer with a beater
attachment as it makes it so quick to do. The usual process is beating
together the butter (whether it is melted, room temperature or cold) and sugar
until combined. Then, the eggs are usually added next, followed by the dry
ingredients, then any flavourings or additions.

You make the cookies huge, or you can make cookies bite-sized. You can eat them
warm and gooey out of the oven, or when they are chilled. Dunk them into some
milk, or tea, or even hot chocolate... there are no rules when it comes to cookies.

Cookies vary between recipes but the main ingredients in this chapter are:

- Unsalted butter
- Sugar (white granulated
  and/or soft brown)
- Eggs
- Vanilla extract

- Plain flour
- Bicarbonate of soda
- Baking powder
- Sea salt

MY TOP TIPS FOR COOKIES:

1 When mixing cookie dough,
try not to overmix... it's an easy
thing to say, but where you are
combining quite a few ingredients
it's easy to get distracted and mix
for too long.

2 If you are rolling your cookie
dough into balls before baking,
try not to roll them too tightly – this
can result in your cookies staying as
mounds rather than flattening down!

3 Not every recipe requires it,
but if the recipe says to chill the
dough... do it! Chilling your cookie

dough is designed to get the
correct shape and end results.

4 You can freeze raw cookie
dough safely for up to 3 months,
and then just bake it whenever you
want a cookie treat! All you need
to do is add 1–2 minutes to your
baking time.

5 How long you bake your
cookies for matters – if you prefer
a softer cookie, take 1–2 minutes
off the baking time, and if you
prefer a chewier/crunchy cookie,
add 1–2 minutes instead.

NYC CHOCOLATE CHIP COOKIES

Makes: 8

Prep: 20 minutes
Chill: 30–60 minutes
Bake: 12–14 minutes
Cool: 30+ minutes
Lasts: 3–4 days, at room temperature

125g unsalted butter
100g soft light brown sugar
75g white granulated sugar
1 egg (medium or large)
1 tsp vanilla extract
300g plain flour
1½ tsp baking powder
½ tsp bicarbonate of soda
½ tsp sea salt
150g dark chocolate chips or chunks
150g milk chocolate chips or chunks

CUSTOMISE:
You can keep the frozen dough in the freezer for up to 3 months. Add 1–2 minutes to the baking time when baking from frozen.

The type of chocolate chips you use is up to you – you can use all dark, all milk or all white or leave them out and add chopped nuts (walnuts, hazelnuts, pecans, pistachios) instead – just make sure the total amount is 300g.

Make a chocolate-flavoured cookie dough using 250g plain flour and 35g cocoa powder.

Giant, gooey and utterly epic, these NYC Chocolate Chip Cookies are based on the famous cookies from New York City. This was one of the most requested recipes on my blog ever, so it had to have a place in this book. I basically wanted to create giant chocolate chip cookies, which are easy to make. The key to these cookies is genuinely – as annoying as this is going to sound – trusting the recipe. They are worth the wait of making the dough, chilling, and letting them cool. You will adore them!

Put the butter and both sugars into a bowl and beat together until creamy. Add the egg and vanilla extract and beat again.

Add the flour, baking powder, bicarbonate of soda and sea salt and mix until a cookie dough is formed. Add the chocolate chips or chunks and mix until well combined.

Portion the dough out into eight balls – they should weigh about 120g each. Once rolled into balls, put the cookie dough in the freezer for at least 30 minutes, or in the fridge for an hour or so.

While the cookie dough is chilling, preheat the oven to 200°C/180°C fan and line two baking trays with parchment paper. Put the cookie dough balls onto the lined baking trays and bake for 12–14 minutes.

Once baked, leave the cookies to cool on the trays for at least 30 minutes as they will continue to bake while cooling.

You can reheat the cookies in the microwave for 20 seconds, or the oven for 2–3 minutes to serve warm.

BROWN BUTTER, PECAN & CHOCOLATE CHIP COOKIES

Makes: 15

Prep: 20 minutes
Chill: 30 minutes
Bake: 10–11 minutes
Cool: 30+ minutes
Lasts: 3–4 days, at room temperature

125g unsalted butter
175g soft light brown sugar
1 egg (medium or large)
1 tsp vanilla extract
275g plain flour
1 tbsp cornflour (optional)
½ tsp bicarbonate of soda
½ tsp sea salt
150g dark chocolate chips
150g pecan nuts, chopped

CUSTOMISE:

You can swap the nuts to any other type of nut you fancy – walnuts, macadamia, etc.

You can use any variety of chocolate chip you like – I just adore the combination of brown butter with pecans and dark chocolate.

The chilling is optional, but can help prevent the cookies spreading too much.

Baking and butter go hand in hand but sometimes it's good to create a new variation. I love brown butter when it comes to cooking dinner, but in baking it's an absolute wonder! It may sound strange, but you melt the butter in a pan, and continue to heat it until it starts to go brown and create a nutty smell. Using this in a cookie creates a whole new layer of flavour that works perfectly with chocolate chips and pecans.

Add the butter to a pan and melt over a medium heat. Keep on heating the butter until it starts to bubble, stirring often so it does not catch. Keep simmering until it starts to smell nutty and turns a brown colour. Pour the butter into a bowl, and leave it to cool to room temperature. It will set back to a softer solid.

Add the browned butter and soft light brown sugar to a bowl and beat until creamy. Add the egg and vanilla extract and beat again. Add the plain flour, cornflour, if using, bicarbonate of soda and salt and mix until a cookie dough is formed. Add the chocolate chips and chopped pecan nuts and stir until evenly distributed.

Portion the cookies into 15 balls, each about 80g. Chill the cookie dough balls in the fridge while you preheat the oven to 200°C/180°C fan and line two baking trays with parchment paper.

Take the cookies out of the fridge, put onto the lined trays and bake for 10–11 minutes. Once baked, leave them to cool on the trays for at least 30 minutes, as they will continue to bake while cooling.

CHOCOLATE ORANGE COOKIES

Makes: 16

Prep: 15 minutes
Bake: 10–11 minutes
Cool: 15+ minutes
Lasts: 4–5 days, at room temperature

125g unsalted butter
100g soft light brown sugar
100g white granulated sugar
1 egg
1 tsp vanilla extract
25g cocoa powder
175g self-raising flour
½ tsp bicarbonate of soda
½ tsp baking powder
½ tsp sea salt
Zest of 1 large orange
250g milk chocolate orange
(I use Terry's), chopped

CUSTOMISE:

I love using milk chocolate orange in these cookies, but you can use dark chocolate, or white! You can also use unflavoured chocolate and add the zest of another orange instead.

The orange zest can be swapped for 1 tsp orange extract.

Make these mint-chocolate flavoured instead – just use unflavoured milk chocolate and 1 tsp peppermint extract.

I have ALWAYS adored chocolate (especially milk chocolate) and orange together. This is the sort of cookie that you will want to bake over and again, partly because it's just so damn easy to make. Honestly, cream the butter and sugars, whack in the egg and vanilla, tip in the dry ingredients, shove in all the orange zest and chocolate and bake. These beauties don't even need chilling – just bake and enjoy!

Preheat the oven to 190°C/170°C fan and line two baking trays with parchment paper.

Put the butter and both sugars in a bowl and beat until creamy. Add the egg and vanilla extract and beat again. Add the cocoa powder, self-raising flour, bicarbonate of soda, baking powder, sea salt and orange zest and mix until a cookie dough is formed.

Add the chopped milk chocolate orange to the cookie dough and mix until evenly distributed, then portion the dough into 16 cookies – I use a 5cm ice-cream scoop for this.

Bake the cookies for 10–11 minutes. Once baked, leave them to cool for at least 15 minutes before devouring – they will still be deliciously warm!

OATMEAL RAISIN COOKIES

Makes: 10

Prep: 20 minutes
Chill: 30–60 minutes
Bake: 10–12 minutes
Cool: 30+ minutes
Lasts: 3–4 days, at room temperature

125g unsalted butter
100g soft light brown sugar
75g white granulated sugar
1 egg (medium or large)
1 tsp vanilla extract
150g plain flour
150g rolled oats
1 tsp baking powder
½ tsp bicarbonate of soda
1 tsp ground cinnamon
½ tsp sea salt
200g raisins

CUSTOMISE:

For smaller cookies rolls the dough into 60g balls and bake for 8–9 minutes.

The raw cookie dough can be frozen for up to 3 months and baked whenever you please – just add 1–2 minutes to the baking time.

The cinnamon is optional, or can be replaced with another flavour such as ground ginger or nutmeg.

The raisins can be combined with 100g chocolate chips, or completely replaced with 300g chocolate chips.

The texture for these is lovely and soft, but the outside is quite chewy – and that's the best thing ever. The raisins give a softer texture, just like you would get with chocolate chips. (Side note: if you don't like raisins, you can use chocolate chips instead!) And like my other cookies, I love the two different sugars in the mix as it gives the best flavour. These cookies are lightly spiced with ground cinnamon for a warming flavour, and are genuinely delicious.

Put the butter and both sugars in a bowl and beat together until creamy. Add the egg and vanilla extract and beat again.

Add the plain flour, rolled oats, baking powder, bicarbonate of soda, ground cinnamon and sea salt and mix until a cookie dough is formed. Mix in the raisins until evenly distributed.

Portion the dough out into 10 balls – they should weigh about 85g each. Don't roll the balls too tightly as this can prevent the cookies spreading. Once rolled, put the balls into the freezer for at least 30 minutes, or in the fridge for an hour or so.

While the cookie dough is chilling, preheat the oven to 200°C/180°C fan and line two baking trays with parchment paper. Take your cookies out of the freezer or fridge and put onto the lined trays (I do five cookies per tray). Bake the cookies for 10–12 minutes.

Once baked, leave the cookies to cool on the trays for at least 30 minutes as they will continue to bake while cooling.

You can reheat the cookies in the microwave for 20 seconds, or the oven for 2–3 minutes to serve warm.

CHOCOLATE VIENNESE WHIRLS

 Makes: 15

Prep: 30 minutes
Bake: 20 minutes
Decorate: 30 minutes
Lasts: 3–4 days, at room temperature

250g unsalted butter, at room
    temperature
75g icing sugar
225g plain flour
25g cocoa powder
30ml full-fat milk

FILLING:
75g unsalted butter, at room
    temperature
150g icing sugar

Viennese whirls are delicate, soft and utterly scrumptious biscuits and I have always adored them… make them chocolate themed, and I love them even more! These may be going against tradition, but they are so beautiful to look at, fun to make, and even better to eat!

Preheat the oven to 180°C/160°C fan and line 2 baking trays with parchment paper.

Beat the butter on its own in a bowl until smooth and creamy. Add the icing sugar to the bowl and mix again until combined. Gradually add the plain flour, cocoa powder and milk until you have a smooth dough.

Spoon the mixture into a piping bag fitted with a star piping tip. Pipe 30 circles of dough, a couple of centimetres apart, onto the lined trays, each one about 5–6cm in diameter. Bake for 20 minutes; once baked, leave to cool on the trays while you make the filling.

Beat the butter in a clean bowl until smooth. Add the icing sugar and beat again until smooth. Pipe or spread a small amount of buttercream filling onto one biscuit and sandwich with another biscuit.

Image on page 9

CUSTOMISE:

The Viennese whirls can be made vanilla flavoured by replacing the cocoa powder with the same amount of plain flour and adding 1 tsp vanilla extract.

Make the buttercream chocolate flavoured by replacing 25g of the icing sugar with cocoa powder.

You can dip the filled or unfilled Viennese whirls in 200g melted chocolate. Leave the biscuits to set on a new lined tray.

S'MORES COOKIES

Makes: 15

Prep: 20 minutes
Chill: 30 minutes–1 hour
Bake: 9–10 minutes
Cool: 30 minutes
Lasts: 3–4 days, at room temperature

300g plain flour
½ tsp baking powder
½ tsp bicarbonate of soda
½ tsp sea salt
175g unsalted butter
150g soft light brown sugar
100g white granulated sugar
1 egg, plus 1 egg yolk
1 tsp vanilla extract
100g biscuits, chopped
200g chocolate chips or chunks
50g mini marshmallows

S'mores are a delicious mixture of chocolate, biscuits and marshmallows. Typically, you would toast marshmallows over a fire and sandwich them between chocolate biscuits – I LOVE THEM. These cookies combine those beautiful flavours into cookie dough. They are soft, gooey and incredibly moreish.

Mix the plain flour, baking powder, bicarbonate of soda and sea salt together in a bowl and leave to the side.

In a separate bowl, beat together the butter and both sugars until creamy. Add the egg, egg yolk and vanilla extract and beat again, then add the dry ingredients and mix until a cookie dough is formed. Finally add the chopped biscuits, chocolate chips or chunks and mini marshmallows and combine until evenly distributed.

Roll the cookie dough into 15 balls and chill in the freezer for at least 30 minutes, or in the fridge for an hour. Meanwhile, preheat the oven to 200°C/180°C fan and line 2–3 baking trays with parchment paper.

Take your cookies out of the freezer or fridge and put onto the lined trays. Bake for 9–10 minutes. Once baked, leave the cookies to cool on the trays for about 5 minutes, then carefully transfer to a wire rack to cool fully.

Image overleaf →

CUSTOMISE:
You can try making stuffed S'mores cookies with 100g extra mini marshmallows. Tightly roll each portion of dough around 5 mini marshmallows and bake as normal.

You can store the dough in the freezer for up to 3 months – add 1–2 minutes to the baking time when baking from frozen.

You can make the cookies chocolate flavoured by replacing 40g of the plain flour with 40g cocoa powder.

SALTED CARAMEL-STUFFED NYC COOKIES

 Makes: 8

Prep: 20 minutes
Chill: 30–60 minutes
Bake: 12–14 minutes
Cool: 30+ minutes
Lasts: 3–4 days, at room temperature

125g unsalted butter
175g soft light brown sugar
1 egg (medium or large)
1 tsp vanilla extract
300g plain flour
1½ tsp baking powder
½ tsp bicarbonate of soda
1 tsp sea salt
250g milk chocolate chips or chunks
8–16 soft caramel sweets

CUSTOMISE:

You can substitute the caramels for spreads, such as chocolate and hazelnut spread or biscuit spread. Simply freeze teaspoons of spread for at least 30 minutes, then wrap the cookie dough around the frozen spread in the same way.

The milk chocolate can be switched to white or dark chocolate.

Make the cookie dough chocolate by using 250g plain flour and adding 35g cocoa powder.

When thinking of cookies, you may think crunchy, or you may think gooey and soft. But do you think a gooey soft centre of caramel? Well, you absolutely should! These cookies have a molten caramel centre that is absolutely incredible, along with a salted cookie dough.

Beat the butter and soft light brown sugar together until creamy. Add the egg and vanilla extract and beat again.

Add the plain flour, baking powder, bicarbonate of soda and sea salt and combine until a cookie dough is formed, then add the chocolate chips or chunks and mix until they are evenly distributed.

Portion your dough out into eight balls – each should weigh about 110g. Once rolled into balls, flatten slightly and put 1 or 2 soft caramels in the middle, then wrap the cookie dough around the caramels and re-roll into balls. Put into the freezer for at least 30 minutes, or in the fridge for an hour or so. While the cookie dough is chilling, preheat the oven to 200°C/180°C fan and line 2 baking trays with parchment paper.

Take your cookies out of the freezer or fridge and put onto the lined trays (I do four cookies per tray) and bake for 12–14 minutes. Once baked, leave the cookies to cool on the trays for at least 30 minutes as they will continue to bake while cooling.

JANE'S SHORTBREAD

♥ **Makes: 16**

Prep: 20 minutes
Bake: 15–18 minutes
Cool: 30+ minutes
Lasts: 4–5 days, at room temperature

175g unsalted butter
75g caster sugar, plus extra for
   sprinkling
260g plain flour, plus extra for dusting
Pinch of salt

FLAVOUR IDEAS (OPTIONAL):
200–300g chocolate chips
   (white/milk/plain)
Zest of 1 lemon
Zest of 1 orange
Zest of 2 limes
75g chopped pistachios, almonds,
   shredded coconut, dried
   cranberries, pecans, walnuts,
   macadamias
1 tbsp dried lavender
1 tsp vanilla extract

CUSTOMISE:

The flavour ideas given above
are just suggestions for what you
can use. Why not experiment by
combining flavours, such as 75g
pecans with 100g chocolate chips?

The shape of the shortbread is also
up to you – I typically choose round
cutters, but squares or rectangles
(or anything else) works too!

I have always loved shortbread and when I was at school it was always my go-to sweet treat. Even now, I LOVE to make this on a regular basis – it's one of those classics that everyone adores (or at least everyone I know). Creaming together the butter and sugar is so easy, then beat in the flour, salt and whatever flavours you fancy and it's done. Honestly, it couldn't be more simple!

Preheat the oven to 190°C/170°C fan and line 2–3 large baking trays with parchment paper.

Cream together the butter and sugar until light and fluffy. Add the plain flour, salt and any flavours you are using and knead the mixture until a dough is formed.

Dust your work surface with a little flour and roll out your dough until it is 1cm thick. Using a 6cm round cutter, cut the cookies out and put onto the lined trays. Gather up the offcuts, re-roll and cut out more rounds – continue until you have used up all the dough (it won't take much kneading to re-roll).

Prick the tops of the shortbreads with a fork and chill in the fridge for at least 30 minutes. Meanwhile, preheat the oven to 180°C/160°C fan.

Bake the chilled shortbread rounds for 15–18 minutes until baked through (they'll be relatively firm). Take the trays out of the oven and sprinkle on some caster sugar. Leave the shortbread to cool on the trays for 5 minutes, then transfer to a wire rack to cool completely.

CARROT CAKE COOKIES

 Makes: 14

Prep: 20 minutes
Bake: 10–12 minutes
Cool: 20 minutes
Lasts: 3–4+ days, at room temperature

125g unsalted butter
150g soft light brown sugar
1 egg (medium or large)
200g finely grated carrot
175g plain flour
75g rolled oats
½ tsp bicarbonate of soda
½ tsp ground cinnamon
1 tsp mixed spice

Carrot cake is one of my favourite cakes, so why not combine the idea with cookies? These are soft, full of flavour and utterly delicious. They are the perfect bake for someone who likes carrot cake and cookies as much as me!

Preheat the oven to 200°C/180°C fan and line 2–3 baking trays with parchment paper.

Add the butter and soft light brown sugar to a bowl and beat together until creamy. Add the egg and finely grated carrot and beat again. Add the flour, oats, bicarbonate of soda, ground cinnamon and mixed spice and mix again.

Spoon the cookie mixture onto the lined trays – I use a 5cm cookie scoop and bake a maximum of 6 cookies per tray. Bake the cookies for 10–12 minutes.

Once baked, leave the cookies to cool on the tray for about 5 minutes, then transfer to a wire rack to cool fully.

CUSTOMISE:

You can sandwich the cookies with a cream cheese frosting to create carrot cake whoopee pies! Beat 50g unsalted butter with 50g icing sugar until smooth, add ½ tsp vanilla extract, 100g full-fat soft cheese and a pinch of ground cinnamon and beat again until combined.

You can add 50g raisins or chopped walnuts to the cookie dough if you like the combination.

The spices are optional, or you can swap and change them to what you prefer such as ground ginger or nutmeg!

WHITE CHOCOLATE BISCOTTI

Makes: 20

Prep: 20 minutes
Bake: 45 minutes
Cool: 1 hour
Lasts: 3–4 days, at room temperature

300g plain flour, plus extra for dusting
100g white granulated sugar
100g soft light brown sugar
1½ tsp baking powder
3 eggs
200g white chocolate chips or chunks

DECORATION (OPTIONAL):
150g white chocolate, melted
5g freeze-dried raspberries
  or 25g nuts, finely chopped

CUSTOMISE:

You can add nuts to the biscotti dough: reduce the amount of white chocolate chips or chunks to 150g and add up to 150g any chopped nut, such as pistachios, hazelnuts, macadamia, walnuts or pecans.

You can swap the white chocolate for milk or dark chocolate.

You can flavour the dough by adding the zest of 1 lemon, or ½ large orange.

Biscotti are quite different to a regular cookies in that they are baked twice, making them super-crunchy and the perfect biscuit to dip into your favourite hot drink. It may sound like these are a bit of work, but they are so worth it and can be tweaked to your ideal flavours. My personal favourite is white chocolate, but honestly... can you blame me?

Preheat the oven to 180°C/160°C fan and line two baking trays with parchment paper.

Mix together the plain flour, both sugars and the baking powder in a large bowl until combined. Beat the eggs together in a separate bowl. Gradually mix the beaten eggs into the dry ingredients a little at a time, mixing fully after each addition. Add the chocolate chips or chunks and mix into the dough.

Turn the dough out onto a lightly floured surface and knead a few times until it is smooth. Split the dough into two even pieces and roll out to form thick but flat logs that are about 4–5cm wide and 2–3cm deep.

Place one on each baking tray and bake for 30 minutes. Once baked, remove from the oven, keep them on the trays, and reduce the oven temperature to 160°C/140°C fan. Leave the biscuit logs for 10–15 minutes until they have cooled slightly.

Slice the logs into individual biscotti, each about 2.5cm thick. Place them back on the trays, cut-side up, and bake for 10–15 minutes until they are dry through. Remove from the oven and leave to cool fully.

If you would like to decorate your biscotti, dip the ends into the melted chocolate and sprinkle with chopped nuts or freeze-dried raspberries.

BREADS
and
Doughnuts

When baking, people tend to think of cakes, cheesecakes, cookies and desserts… but one of the most satisfying things to bake is breads and doughnuts.

Most people do think of bread as savoury, but when you get into the world of cinnamon rolls, babka, or even lemon and raspberry rolls you will find so much baking joy because they are all SO YUMMY. This chapter has some absolutely stunning sweet breads, along with some of my favourite doughnut recipes.

This chapter is probably the most lengthy because every bake takes a few hours, but trust me… they are worth the time and effort. Baking bread can be very simple, and therapeutic. The kneading times given in the following recipes are based on using a stand mixer with a dough hook so if you are kneading by hand it will take a few minutes longer, but it is totally worth it! It often takes much longer for doughs to prove in winter because the temperature of your kitchen is colder, and in the peak summer it can take a fraction of the time.

The best flour to use when baking bread or doughnuts is strong white bread flour as it creates the best structure, but most of the time it can be switched to plain flour. As long as you have yeast, you will be fine.

The main ingredients I use in this chapter are:

- Strong white bread flour
- Yeast
- Sugar
- Milk
- Unsalted butter
- Eggs
- Plus any flavourings

MY TOP TIPS FOR BREADS & DOUGHNUTS:

1 Doughnuts can be quite scary, as most of the time for a classic doughnut you need to fry them. Investing in a kitchen thermometer that you can use for the oil means you can create baking wonders.

2 Be patient when it comes to proving times – sometimes it can be quick, sometimes it can take a while. If you underprove your dough, you won't get nearly as delicious results!

3 Similarly don't overprove your dough – typically you want the dough to double in size.

4 Don't worry if you don't have a stand mixer with a dough hook; you can easily make bread with a bowl and your hands. Just be patient and keep kneading until you have a smooth dough that springs back!

CINNAMON ROLLS

Makes: 12

Prep: 3–4 hours
Prove: 2–3 hours
Bake: 20–25 minutes
Cool: 30+ minutes
Lasts: 2–3 days, at room temperature

600g strong white bread flour,
  plus extra for dusting
75g caster sugar
14g dried yeast
90g chilled unsalted butter, cubed
275ml full-fat milk
1 tsp vanilla extract
1 egg (medium or large)

FILLING:
175g soft light brown sugar
1–2 tbsp ground cinnamon
40g unsalted butter, melted

TOPPING:
300g icing sugar
1 tsp vanilla extract
3–4 tbsp water

Cinnamon rolls are one of those bakes that I like to pick up when I am at a coffee shop or bakery – especially if they are warm and fresh out of the oven. But whenever I do this I find myself wanting more. I also find whoever I am with wanting more too… so why not bake an entire batch? Cinnamon is a very Christmassy spice, but my gosh I just adore it all the time. These cinnamon rolls are heaven in a bite and it's a popular recipe on my blog, too. I make sure that my cinnamon rolls are quite thick with cinnamon goodness, but that's entirely your choice.

Sift the flour into a large bowl, add the caster sugar and dried yeast and mix together. Rub the butter into the mixture until it resembles breadcrumbs.

Gently heat the milk in a small pan until warm but not piping hot – it should just be starting to steam. Add the warm milk, vanilla extract and egg to the dry ingredients and start mixing. Knead the dough for 7–10 minutes; it will be sticky at first, but it will soon come together. Once kneaded, it will be springy to touch, and not sticky.

Transfer the ball of dough to a clean, lightly oiled bowl, cover the top with clingfilm and leave the dough to rise for 1–2 hours, or until doubled in size.

While the bread is proving, whisk together the light brown sugar and cinnamon for the filling and set aside.

Continued overleaf →

CUSTOMISE:

If you would like to serve the cinnamon rolls for breakfast, you can do the second prove in the fridge overnight, so you can bake them fresh in the morning.

You can use a cream cheese frosting for the topping instead for extra indulgence. Use the recipe from my Red Velvet Cupcakes (see page 77).

If you would like to use fresh yeast, you will need 28g.

Some yeasts need activating (check the packet). If so, add the yeast to the warm milk.

If you don't like cinnamon, you can use other flavours such as ground ginger or nutmeg.

You can add chocolate chips to the dough by sprinkling 175g chocolate chips on top of the cinnamon sugar before you roll up the dough.

You can use plain flour instead of strong white bread flour – the texture will just be slightly more cakey.

Once the dough has risen, transfer to a lightly floured work surface and roll out to a large rectangle – about 50 x 30cm. Gently brush the surface with the melted butter and then sprinkle over the sugar/cinnamon mix. Roll the dough up quite tightly from long side to long side, then, using a sharp knife, cut this evenly into 12 pieces.

Put the pieces into a large rectangular baking dish (mine was roughly 30 x 24cm), cover the dish with clingfilm and let the rolls rise for another hour or so. By the end, they should all be touching. Towards the end of this second prove, preheat the oven to 180°C/160°C fan.

Bake the rolls for 20–25 minutes until golden brown and cooked through. Leave to cool for at least 30 minutes while you make the topping. Simply whisk all the ingredients together until a thick icing paste is formed. Spread or drizzle over the rolls.

CHOCOLATE CHERRY BABKA

 Makes: 8

Prep: 3–4 hours
Prove: 1½ hours
Bake: 50–60 minutes
Cool: 1 hour
Lasts: 2–3 days, at room temperature

150g strong white bread flour,
   plus extra for dusting
150g plain flour
25g caster sugar
7g dried yeast
75g chilled unsalted butter, cubed
125ml full-fat milk
1 egg

FILLING:
40g unsalted butter, plus extra
   for greasing
40g soft light brown sugar
75g dark chocolate, chopped
25g cocoa powder
200g pitted cherries, halved

GLAZE:
50g caster sugar
50ml water

Babka has always fascinated me as it's just so beautiful to look at – just look at the swirls and patterns in the bake! It's deceptively easy to make, and always has absolutely winning results. This one is Black Forest-inspired with the chocolate filling and cherries, but you can easily chop and change it. It's 100 per cent worth the proving time – so much so that you'll want to experiment and make it over and over again!

Sift both flours into a large bowl, add the caster sugar and dried yeast and mix together. Rub the butter into the mixture until it resembles breadcrumbs.

Gently heat the milk in a small pan until warm but not piping hot – it should just be starting to steam. Mix the warm milk and egg into the dry ingredients. Knead the dough together for 7 minutes; it will be sticky at first, but it will soon come together. Once kneaded, it should be springy to touch, and not sticky.

Transfer the dough to a clean, lightly oiled bowl, cover the top of the bowl with clingfilm and let the dough rise for 1 hour, or until doubled in size.

Meanwhile, prepare the filling. Heat the butter and soft light brown sugar in a pan and stir until melted. Reduce the heat to low and add the chopped dark chocolate and cocoa powder. Stir until the chocolate has melted and mixture is combined – it might look grainy, but that is fine.

Once the dough has risen, transfer to a lightly floured work surface, and roll out to a rectangle about 40 x 30cm. Gently brush the surface with the chocolate filling, then sprinkle over the cherries.

Continued overleaf →

CHOCOLATE CHERRY BABKA
CONTINUED

CUSTOMISE:
The cherries can be left out for
a chocolate babka – or you can
flavour the filling with the zest of
1 large orange, 1 tsp peppermint
extract or 1 tsp coffee extract.

You can also flavour the dough
with the flavourings above.

If you want an extra kick, you can
swap the fresh cherries for cherries
soaked in kirsch out of a jar!

Roll the dough up quite tightly from long side to long side until it is a long sausage shape. Carefully cut the dough lengthways down the middle. Twist the two halves around each other until fully twisted into a sort of two-strand plait. Place the twisted dough into a lightly buttered 900g loaf tin, making sure the dough is level and not sticking up at the sides. Cover the tin loosely with clingfilm and leave the babka to rise for another 30 minutes or so. Towards the end of this second prove, preheat the oven to 180°C/160°C fan.

Bake for 50–60 minutes until golden brown. Cool the babka in the tin for at least 10 minutes, and then carefully remove and cool fully on a wire rack while you make the glaze.

Heat the caster sugar and water in a small pan until the sugar has dissolved. Leave the mixture to cool slightly and brush over the babka.

CHELSEA BUNS

♥ **Makes: 12–14**

Prep: 3–4 hours
Prove: 2–3 hours
Bake: 20–25 minutes
Cool: 30+ minutes
Lasts: 2–3 days, at room temperature

600g strong white bread flour,
   plus extra for dusting
75g caster sugar
14g dried yeast
90g chilled unsalted butter, cubed
275ml full-fat milk
1 tsp vanilla extract
Zest of 1–2 lemons
1 egg (medium or large)

FILLING:
40g unsalted butter, melted
75g soft light brown sugar
200g mixed dried fruit

TOPPING:
2–3 tbsp honey
2 tbsp demerara sugar (optional)

CUSTOMISE:
You can use sultanas, raisins or any other dried fruit you fancy.

You can use golden syrup for the glaze, or make a simple sugar syrup by melting 2 tbsp caster sugar with 2 tbsp water in a pan.

A variation on cinnamon rolls, these are light, fruity and the perfect bake. Pack the fresh, lemony dough full of dried fruits and finish with a sticky honey glaze. Delicious served warm, these are ideal for those who love to have a bit of fun with their baking.

Sift the flour into a large bowl, add the caster sugar and dried yeast and mix together. Rub the butter into the mixture until it resembles breadcrumbs.

Gently heat the milk in a small pan until warm but not piping hot – it should just be starting to steam. Mix the warm milk, vanilla extract, lemon zest and egg into the dry ingredients. Knead the dough together for 7–10 minutes – it will be sticky at first, but it will soon come together. Once kneaded, it will be springy to touch, and not sticky.

Transfer the dough to a clean, lightly oiled bowl, cover the top with clingfilm and leave to rise for 1–2 hours, or until doubled in size.

Once the dough has risen, transfer to a lightly floured work surface, and roll out to a large rectangle about 50 x 30cm. Gently brush the surface with the melted butter, then sprinkle over the soft light brown sugar and the mixed dried fruit. Roll the dough up quite tightly from long side to long side and then use a sharp knife to cut this evenly into 12–14 pieces.

Arrange the pieces evenly in a large dish – I use a 30cm round dish. Cover the dish with clingfilm, and let the rolls rise for another hour or so. By the end, they should all be touching. Towards the end of this second prove, preheat the oven to 180°C/160°C fan.

Bake for 20–25 minutes until golden brown and cooked through. Once out of the oven, carefully melt the honey slightly in a pan. Brush the honey over the tops of the buns and sprinkle over the demerara sugar, if using. Leave them to cool for at least 30 minutes before devouring.

CHOCOLATE RASPBERRY ROLLS

♥ Makes: 6–8

Prep: 3–4 hours
Prove: 2–3 hours
Bake: 20–25 minutes
Cool: 30+ minutes
Lasts: 2–3 days, at room temperature

280g strong white bread flour,
   plus extra for dusting
20g cocoa powder
7g dried yeast
35g caster sugar
45g chilled unsalted butter, cubed
150ml full-fat milk
½ tsp vanilla extract
1 egg
75g white chocolate chips
75g dark chocolate chips

FILLING:

25g unsalted butter, melted
50g soft light brown sugar
   (or caster sugar)
100g frozen raspberries

CUSTOMISE:
I use frozen raspberries because
when they thaw during baking,
they produce a delicious sticky
raspberry sauce. You can use fresh
raspberries instead.

The chocolate chips in the dough
are optional – they can be added
into the filling instead.

You can decorate the rolls by
drizzling over 75g melted chocolate.

**Why would you not want to combine chocolate, raspberries
and delicious bread in a warm, cosy and gooey bake?!
These chocolate and raspberry rolls are sweet, chocolatey
and splendid.**

Sift the flour and cocoa powder into a large bowl, add the
caster sugar and dried yeast and mix together. Rub the
butter into the mixture until it resembles breadcrumbs.

Gently heat the milk in a small pan until warm but not piping
hot – it should just be starting to steam. Mix the warm milk,
vanilla extract and egg yolk into the dry ingredients. Knead
the dough together for 3 minutes, then add the chocolate
chips. Continue kneading for a further 3 minutes.

Transfer the dough to a clean, lightly oiled bowl, cover the
top of the bowl with clingfilm and let the dough rise for
2 hours, or until doubled in size at least.

Once the dough has risen, transfer to a lightly floured
work surface, and roll out to a rectangle about 30 x 20cm.
Gently brush the surface with the melted butter, then sprinkle
over the caster sugar and frozen raspberries. Roll the dough
up quite tightly from long side to long side and cut this roll
evenly into 6–8 pieces.

Arrange the buns in a dish that is roughly 17 x 24cm in
size. Cover the dish with clingfilm, and let them rise for
another hour or so. By the end, they should all be touching.
Towards the end of this second prove, preheat the oven to
180°C/160°C fan.

Bake for 20–25 minutes until firm to the touch. Leave to
cool in the tin for at least 30 minutes before tucking in
and enjoying.

STICKY CARAMEL PECAN ROLLS

 Makes: 6–8

Prep: 3–4 hours
Prove: 2–3 hours
Bake: 20–25 minutes
Cool: 30 minutes
Lasts: 2–3 days, at room temperature

300g strong white bread flour,
**   plus extra for dusting**
7g dried yeast
35g caster sugar
45g chilled unsalted butter, cubed
150ml full-fat milk
½ tsp vanilla extract
1 egg

CARAMEL SAUCE:
175g soft light brown sugar
100g unsalted butter
½ tsp vanilla extract
75ml double cream

FILLING:
25g unsalted butter, melted
50g soft light brown sugar
125g pecans, chopped

A batch of sticky caramel pecan rolls… honestly, what could be better? Homemade caramel sauce with fresh and light rolls stuffed with a brown sugar pecan filling! They are gooey, cosy and delicious in every bite.

Sift the flour into a large bowl, add the caster sugar and dried yeast and mix together. Rub the butter into the mixture until it resembles breadcrumbs.

Gently heat the full-fat milk in a small pan until warm but not piping hot – it should just be starting to steam. Mix the warm milk, vanilla extract and egg into the dry ingredients. Knead the dough together for 5–7 minutes – it will be sticky at first, but it will soon come together. Once kneaded, it will be springy to touch, and not sticky.

Transfer the dough to a clean, lightly oiled bowl, cover the top of the bowl with clingfilm and let the dough rise for 1–2 hours, or until doubled in size.

While the dough is proving, make the caramel sauce. Add all of the sauce ingredients to a medium pan and melt over a medium heat, stirring until it reaches a dark brown colour and the mixture is smooth. Leave the caramel to cool.

Once the dough has risen, transfer to a lightly floured work surface, and roll out to a rectangle about 30 x 20cm. Gently brush the surface with the melted butter. Sprinkle over the soft light brown sugar and the chopped pecans. Roll the dough up quite tightly from long side to long side, then cut this evenly into 6–8 pieces.

The pecans can be swapped for raisins, or mixed dried fruit, or any other nut such as walnuts, macadamias or even pistachios.

You can use shop-bought caramel sauce if you prefer, but this homemade one is just lovely!

The recipe can be doubled and baked in a large 30cm round dish if you want a larger batch.

Pour the caramel sauce into a small baking dish about 20cm square. Evenly arrange the pecan buns on top of the sauce, leaving space in between the buns for them to grow. Cover the dish with clingfilm, and let them rise for another hour or so. By the end, they should all be touching. Towards the end of this second prove, preheat the oven to 180°C/160°C fan.

Bake for about 20–25 minutes until golden brown and cooked through and the caramel sauce is bubbling up. Once out of the oven, either serve from the dish and scoop up the caramel sauce, or turn the buns out onto a new serving dish (so that the caramel bottom becomes the top) and have the caramel sauce on top.

Image overleaf →

GLAZED RING DOUGHNUTS

Makes: 12

Prep: 3–4 hours
Prove: 1½–3 hours
Fry: 20–30 minutes
Lasts: 1–2 days (but best served fresh)

450g strong white bread flour,
   plus extra for dusting
50g caster sugar
½ tsp salt
14g dried yeast
75g chilled unsalted butter, cubed
200ml full-fat milk
1 tsp vanilla extract
2 eggs
2 litres sunflower oil, for frying

TOPPING IDEAS:
400g icing sugar + 2–3 tbsp water,
   with 15g freeze-dried raspberries
400g icing sugar + 2–3 tbsp water,
   with 150g sprinkles
400g chocolate, with chocolate curls

I love doughnuts. I always have, and I always will. They take a bit of time and patience, but they have the fluffiest and softest texture with a lightly crispy outside. These are so fun to make and decorate – you can top the doughnuts with whatever you want (just take a look at the glazed ring doughnuts on my blog), such as chocolate, icing, sprinkles etc!

Sift the flour into a large bowl, add the caster sugar, salt and yeast and mix together. With your fingertips, rub butter into the mixture until it resembles breadcrumbs.

Gently heat the milk until warm but not piping hot. If heating in a pan, you want it to just start steaming. Mix the warm milk, vanilla extract and eggs into the dry ingredients with a spatula to bring the mixture together.

Knead the dough together for 7–10 minutes. It will be sticky at first, but it will soon come together. Once kneaded, it will be springy to touch, and not sticky.

Transfer the dough to a clean, lightly oiled bowl, cover with clingfilm and set aside to rise for 1–2 hours, or until doubled in size.

Once the dough has risen, roll it out on a lightly floured work surface until it is 2cm thick. Using a 9cm round cutter, cut out as many doughnut shapes as you can, then use a 4cm round cutter to cut out the middle of each round to form a ring. Re-roll the dough and repeat to make 12 doughnuts in total.

Line a large baking tray with parchment paper, lightly dust with flour and arrange the doughnuts on the tray. Cover with a lightly oiled piece of clingfilm and leave to prove again for 30–60 minutes, or until doubled in size.

Pour the oil into a wide, high-sided pan to a depth of about 5cm and heat until the oil reaches a temperature of 170°C – test this with a thermometer.

CUSTOMISE:

The doughnuts can be made bigger or smaller – you just need to adjust the frying time. Keep an eye on the colour and do a test doughnut if needed.

The doughnut holes can be fried on their own for 30 seconds each side, and then coated in caster sugar for a nice treat.

You can decorate or top these with whatever you fancy – these are just my favourite suggestions.

Carefully lower the doughnuts into the oil with a slotted spoon, two at a time, and fry for 1–2 minutes each side. The doughnuts should turn a nice golden colour – if they are browning very quickly it's because the oil is too hot so remove the pan from the heat. Once the doughnuts are golden all over, remove carefully from the oil, and drain on a tray lined with kitchen paper. Repeat until all the doughnuts are done.

Decorate your doughnuts in one of the following ways:

FREEZE-DRIED RASPBERRIES:
In a bowl, mix together the icing sugar and water until you have a thick paste. Dunk the doughnuts into the icing and place on a tray. Sprinkle with freeze-dried raspberries and leave to set.

SPRINKLE DOUGHNUTS:
In a bowl, mix together the icing sugar and water until you have a thick paste. Pour the sprinkles into a separate bowl. Dunk the doughnuts into the icing and then dunk straight into the sprinkles. Turn over, and put on a tray to set.

CHOCOLATE:
Melt the chocolate in a heatproof bowl (I do this in a microwave). Dunk the doughnuts into the chocolate, and then place on a tray. Sprinkle with chocolate curls.

DOUGHNUT BITES

 Makes: 15

Prep: 30 minutes
Fry: 20 minutes
Lasts: 1–2 days (but best served fresh)

250g plain flour, plus extra for dusting
50g caster sugar
2 tsp baking powder
Pinch of salt
75g chilled unsalted butter, cubed
150ml full-fat milk
1 litre sunflower oil, for frying

COATING:
100g caster sugar

Doughnut bites (or doughnut holes) are usually something that gets ignored, especially if you have a freshly made, delicious, sweet doughnut staring straight at you. However these are designed to be doughnut bites. These sweet mini doughnuts, coated in sugar, are the best and because they use a slightly different dough (no bread flour, yeast or proving time), they are quick to make and even quicker to eat!

Add the plain flour, caster sugar, baking powder and salt to a bowl and mix to combine. With your fingertips, rub the butter into the mixture until it resembles breadcrumbs. Slowly add the milk to the bowl, mixing with a spatula or your hands, until a dough is formed.

Turn the dough out on to a lightly floured work surface and knead until you have a ball that is smooth and not too sticky.

Pour the oil in a large pan and heat until it reaches about 170°C – test this with a thermometer.

While the oil is heating, portion the dough into about 15 balls (about 1 tablespoon of dough each) and roll into mini doughnuts.

Carefully lower the doughnut bites into the oil with a slotted spoon, about 4 or 5 at a time, and fry about 1–2 minutes on each side. Once the doughnuts are a lovely golden colour, transfer them to a tray lined with kitchen paper to soak up any excess oil and then toss each doughnut bite into the caster sugar. Enjoy while still warm.

CUSTOMISE:
You can flavour the doughnuts by adding ½ tsp ground cinnamon, nutmeg or ginger, or ½ tsp vanilla extract to the dough.

You can flavour the sugar coating by adding 1 tsp ground cinnamon.

CHOCOLATE CHEESECAKE DOUGHNUTS

❤ **Makes: 6–7**

Prep: 3–4 hours
Prove: 1½–3 hours
Fry: 20–30 minutes
Cool: 30 minutes
Lasts: 1–2 days (but best served fresh)

200g strong white bread flour,
   plus extra for dusting
25g cocoa powder
25g caster sugar
Pinch of salt
7g dried yeast
35g chilled unsalted butter, cubed
100ml full-fat milk
½ tsp vanilla extract
1 egg
2 litres sunflower oil, for frying

COATING:
100g caster sugar

FILLING:
150g full-fat soft cheese
25g icing or caster sugar
75ml double cream
½ tsp vanilla extract

Why not combine several of my favourite things in one bake? Doughnuts, chocolate and cheesecake come together to create an absolutely indulgent creation: soft chocolate-flavoured doughnut filled with vanilla cheesecake and coated in sugar. You will struggle to only eat one of these as they are totally heavenly and can easily be customised to whatever flavours you prefer!

Sift the flour and cocoa powder into a large bowl, add the caster sugar, salt and yeast and mix together. With your fingertips, rub the butter into the mixture until it resembles breadcrumbs.

Gently heat the milk until warm but not piping hot; it should just be starting to steam. Pour the warm milk, vanilla extract and egg into the dry ingredients and mix with a spatula to bring it together. Knead the dough together for 5–7 minutes – it will be sticky at first, but it will soon come together. Once kneaded, it will be springy to touch, and not sticky.

Transfer the dough to a clean, lightly oiled bowl, cover with clingfilm and set aside to rise for 1–2 hours, or until doubled in size.

Once the dough has risen, take it out of the bowl and knock the dough back by kneading briefly. Split the mixture evenly into 6–7 pieces, then roll into balls on a work surface until smooth.

Line a baking tray with parchment paper, lightly dust with flour and then arrange the doughnuts on the tray. Loosely cover with a lightly oiled piece of clingfilm and leave to prove again for 30–60 minutes, or until doubled in size.

CUSTOMISE:

The doughnut mixture can be made plain by replacing the cocoa powder with another 25g of strong white bread flour.

The cheesecake mixture can be flavoured easily by adding any of the following:

- 25g salted caramel sauce
- 15g cocoa powder
- ½ tsp orange/peppermint/ coffee extract

The cheesecake filling can also be swapped to any chocolate spread or jam.

If you have an air fryer you can bake these instead; simply set the temperature to 170°C on the cake setting and fry for 6 minutes. You'll need to coat the doughnuts in a little melted butter so that the sugar will stick.

Pour the oil into a wide, high-sided pan to a depth of about 5cm and heat to 170°C – test this with a thermometer. Carefully lower the doughnuts into the hot oil with a slotted spoon, two at a time, and fry for 1–2 minutes on each side, until the doughnuts turn a nice golden colour. If they are browning too quickly, remove the pan from the heat.

Once the doughnuts are golden all over, carefully remove from the oil and drain on some kitchen paper. Pour the caster sugar into a bowl and carefully turn each doughnut in the sugar until coated. Leave the doughnuts to cool on a tray while you make the filling.

Put all the filling ingredients in a bowl and whisk together until smooth and thick, then transfer to a disposable piping bag. Use a knife to pierce a small hole in the side of each doughnut, then snip off a small amount of the end of the piping bag. Start piping the cheesecake mixture into the doughnuts – you will feel the doughnut get heavier, and when it's full the mixture will reach the hole. Repeat until all the doughnuts are filled. Enjoy!

Image overleaf →

BAKED CINNAMON SUGAR DOUGHNUTS

Makes: 16

Prep: 20 minutes
Bake: 10–13 minutes
Cool: 30 minutes
Lasts: 2–3 days (but best served fresh)

150g unsalted butter
150g caster sugar
1 large egg
175g plain flour
1 tsp baking powder
½ tsp ground cinnamon
¼ tsp salt
100ml full-fat milk
1 tsp vanilla extract

COATING:
125g caster sugar
2 tsp ground cinnamon

These baked doughnuts are light, covered in cinnamon sugar and got a rapturous response on my blog. The mixture is similar to a cake batter, which you bake into mini doughnut moulds and then cover in sugar when they are out of the oven. They are so wonderful! Serve them with some melted chocolate to dip into, or just enjoy them as they are.

Preheat the oven to 180°C/160°C fan and grease a mini-doughnut mould tray.

Put the butter and caster sugar in a large bowl and cream together until smooth. Add the egg and beat again.

In a separate bowl, whisk together the plain flour, baking powder, cinnamon and salt. In another bowl, whisk together the milk and vanilla extract. Add half of the flour mixture and half of the milk mixture to the butter/sugar mixture and beat until smooth. Add the remaining halves of both mixtures and beat again until combined.

Transfer the mixture to a large piping bag and then pipe the mixture into the moulds (my doughnut mould tray has six holes so I pipe and bake these in three batches). You want the mixture to be level with the middle of the doughnut hole in the mould so that it doesn't overflow during baking.

CUSTOMISE:

The cinnamon can be left out, or swapped for a different flavour such as ground ginger.

The doughnuts can be made chocolate themed by replacing 25g of the plain flour with cocoa powder.

I recommend serving the doughnuts with 100g melted chocolate for dipping.

If you don't want to use a mini doughnut mould, split the mixture between 16 cupcake cases, and bake for about 15 minutes. Remove from the cases and cover in the cinnamon sugar.

Bake the doughnuts for 10–13 minutes. They should be an even colour, firm to the touch and not making a bubbly sound. Once baked, take the mould tray out the oven, and turn upside down on to a wire rack and leave for 2 minutes. Meanwhile, in a separate bowl, whisk together the caster sugar and the ground cinnamon for the sugar coating.

Once the doughnuts having been cooling upside down for 2 minutes, carefully remove the doughnuts from the moulds, toss each one in the cinnamon sugar and leave to cool on another wire rack.

Repeat the process until all of the mixture has been used up.

Tray-bakes

Anyone who knows me knows that I love making traybakes. There are so many options with them, and they are ALWAYS a hit with anyone who you bake them for. Ideal for sharing with friends and family, they are the perfect bake for a special occasion and ideal for bake sales.

When I think back to when I was first baking as a kid, I can remember making brownies and wanting to lick the spoon because the chocolate mix looked so good! Whenever people brought cakes to school, everyone always wanted the flapjack, or the rocky road – traybakes are the best! Brownies, flapjacks, rocky road, blondies, no-bake slices, cookie bars... honestly the list is endless and I adore them all.

There are so many ingredients you can use when it comes to traybakes – all of the obvious ones such as sugar, butter, flour and eggs, but you can also use oats, mini marshmallows, chocolate chips, almonds, jam etc. As you know, I love a variation, and all of these recipes are so easy to customise to what you love.

Whether you stick to one of the basic recipes in this chapter or use one of the alternative ideas, you'll soon find out that once you have the basics sorted, you can do so much more.

MY TOP TIPS FOR TRAYBAKES:

1 Make sure you use the correct size tray – I always bake my traybakes in a 23cm square tin, as it's so easy to cut them into 16 pieces, but all of the recipes also work in a 18 x 27cm tin as the volume of the two are about the same.

2 A lot of these recipes rely on the fridge for some part of the recipe, and it's worth it! Chilling bakes can be painful when you want to dive into the deliciousness that you have just made, but trust in the process!

3 Always line your trays with parchment paper as this will make it much easier to get the bake out of the tin – especially when there's chocolate or caramel involved!

4 All of the recipes freeze well – I find it's best to portion up after baking and then freeze in a freezerproof container or bag so you can enjoy them as and when you please!

5 If you want to make a half batch of a recipe, use an 18cm square tin instead of a 23cm square tin and reduce the baking time.

6 Flavour your brownies with nuts, fruit or chocolate and make your flapjacks fruity or coconut flavoured – experiment with the flavours and ingredients you love best! Chocolate chips, chocolate chunks, chopped up bars of chocolate... they all work well!

TRIPLE CHOCOLATE BROWNIES

Makes: 16

Prep: 20 minutes
Bake: 25–30 minutes
Cool: 1 hour
Lasts: 4–5+ days, at room temperature

200g unsalted butter
200g dark chocolate
4 eggs
275g caster sugar
100g plain flour
50g cocoa powder
100g white chocolate chips
100g milk chocolate chips
100g dark chocolate chips

CUSTOMISE:
The brownies can be flavoured with vanilla extract, peppermint extract, or the zest of a large orange.

You can also fold through pieces of your favourite chocolate bars – soft-centred bars should be frozen before baking into brownies, but solid chocolate bars can be baked straight away!

You can also add any of the following to your brownies:
· 200g dried fruit or nuts
· 150g frozen or fresh berries
· 75g desiccated coconut

I utterly adore brownies that are absolutely full of chocolate flavour. These are thick, fudgy and gooey all at once – perfection! I always use dark chocolate with at least 70% cocoa solids for brownies as it creates the BEST flavour – this is another recipe that has a firm following on my blog so you obviously all agree! With this rich delicious base, I flavour my brownies with three types of chocolate chips – but you can choose whatever you want. And the great thing about brownies is that you can warm them up, top with ice cream and enjoy as a pudding!

Preheat the oven to 180°C/160°C fan and line a 23cm square baking tin with parchment paper.

Melt together the butter and dark chocolate in a heatproof bowl set over a pan of simmering water, or in the microwave for 1–2 minutes. Set aside to cool to room temperature.

Using an electric whisk or stand mixer, whisk together the eggs and caster sugar for a few minutes until the colour has turned pale, is very mousse-like, and has doubled in volume. You will know when it's ready because when you lift the whisk out of the mix it should leave a trail for a couple of seconds before disappearing.

Pour the cooled chocolate and butter over the egg and sugar mixture and fold together carefully. It might take some time but be patient – you do not want to knock out the air you whisked in at the previous step. Once completely combined, sift the plain flour and cocoa powder on top of the chocolate mix and then gently fold together again. Fold through the chocolate chips and pour into the lined tin.

Bake for 25–30 minutes. Once baked, leave to cool fully in the tin. You can also 'set' the brownies in the fridge for 2 hours to create a lovely fudgy texture once they have cooled from the oven.

STICKY TOFFEE BROWNIES

♥ **Makes: 16**

Prep: 45 minutes
Bake: 25–30 minutes
Cool: 1 hour
Lasts: 4–5+ days, at room temperature

TOFFEE SAUCE:
10ml double cream
1 tbsp black treacle
50g soft dark brown sugar
35g unsalted butter

BROWNIES:
200g unsalted butter
200g dark chocolate
4 eggs
250g soft dark brown sugar
100g plain flour
50g cocoa powder
100g pitted dates, chopped
100g chocolate chips
100g toffee sauce (see above)

CUSTOMISE:
The black treacle in the toffee sauce can be swapped for golden syrup if you prefer a lighter flavour.

The soft dark brown sugar can be swapped for soft light brown sugar for a lighter flavour.

The chopped dates are optional – they can be left out, or swapped for more chocolate chips.

You can use shop-bought toffee sauce if you prefer.

Brownies are always deliciously chocolatey – and rightly so. But why not bake them with something else that is delicious and cosy and epic? These sticky toffee brownies combine a homemade sticky toffee sauce with a fudgy brownie mixture, creating an absolute explosion of deliciousness.

First make the toffee sauce. Put all of the ingredients into a pan, place over a low-medium heat and stir until the sugar has dissolved and the butter has melted. Bring to the boil and stir for 1–2 minutes so it thickens slightly. Set aside to cool while you make the brownies.

Preheat the oven to 180°C/160°C fan and line a 23cm square baking tin with parchment paper.

Melt together the butter and dark chocolate in a heatproof bowl set over a pan of simmering water (bain-marie), or in the microwave for 1–2 minutes. Set aside to cool to room temperature.

Whisk together the eggs and brown sugar in a separate bowl for a few minutes until the colour has turned lighter and the mixture leaves a trail for a couple of seconds. Pour the cooled chocolate mix over the eggs and fold together carefully until completely combined, then sift in the plain flour and cocoa powder and gently fold together again. Once well combined, fold through the chopped dates and chocolate chips.

Pour the mixture into the lined tin, then spoon over the toffee sauce and swirl it slightly through the mixture. Bake for 25–30 minutes, then remove from the oven and leave to cool fully in the tin. You can 'set' the brownies in the fridge for 2 hours to create a lovely fudgy texture once they have cooled from the oven.

136 TRAYBAKES

BAKEWELL BLONDIES

Makes: 16

Prep: 15 minutes
Bake: 30–35 minutes
Cool: 2 hours
Lasts: 1+ week, at room temperature

250g unsalted butter, melted
125g white granulated sugar
125g soft light brown sugar
3 eggs
1 tsp almond extract
200g plain flour
100g ground almonds
1 tbsp cornflour
200g white chocolate chips or chunks
250g raspberry jam
50g flaked almonds

Almond and jam… a delicious combination. Usually in a Bakewell slice there is a pastry base, a jam layer, and almond filling, and decoration on top. These blondies from my blog basically use the same flavours, just without the pastry! I've used raspberry jam, but you can use whatever jam you fancy – strawberry is my second favourite, along with cherry.

Preheat the oven to 180°C/160°C fan and line a 23cm square tin with parchment paper.

Beat the melted butter, white granulated sugar and soft light brown sugar in a large bowl until smooth. Add the eggs and almond extract and beat again until smooth.

Add the plain flour, ground almonds and cornflour and beat until you have a thick blondie mixture, then add the white chocolate chips and fold through.

Pour the mixture into the tin, and spread evenly. Dollop on the jam using a teaspoon, and lightly swirly through the blondie mixture. Finally sprinkle over the flaked almonds.

Bake the blondies for 30–35 minutes, or until there is an ever so slight wobble in the middle. Leave to cool fully in the tin before cutting into squares.

CUSTOMISE:

The raspberry jam can be swapped to any flavour you like – strawberry and cherry are delicious alternatives.

The almond extract can be left out or, if you love almond flavour, you can increase it to 2 tsp.

The white chocolate chips or chunks can be swapped for milk or dark chocolate, or even left out.

FLAPJACKS

 Makes: 16

Prep: 15 minutes
Bake: 20–25 minutes
Cool: 1 hour
Lasts: 1+ week, at room temperature

200g unsalted butter
200g demerara sugar or soft light
   brown sugar
200g golden syrup
400g rolled oats

CUSTOMISE:
You can flavour the flapjacks
with any, or a combination of the
following:

- 1 tsp ground cinnamon
- 1 tsp ground ginger
- 1 tsp vanilla extract
- Zest of 1 lemon
- Zest of 1 orange

You can add any of these to
the oats:

- 100g dried fruits (such as raisins,
  sultanas, mixed fruit)
- 100g nuts (such as walnuts,
  pecans, macadamias)
- 50g desiccated coconut
- 100g chocolate chips or chunks

Honey makes a great alternative
to the golden syrup.

When I think of flapjacks, I think of delicious and kind-of-sticky traybakes, full of oats and utterly delicious. My base recipe has four simple ingredients – unsalted butter, sugar, oats and syrup – golden syrup creates such a good flavour. Also, the amazing thing about flapjacks is that you can customise them so easily with flavourings, such as fruits, chocolate – you name it!

Preheat the oven to 180°C/160°C fan and line a 23cm square tin with parchment paper.

Put the butter, sugar and syrup into a medium pan and melt over a low heat until smooth.

Put the rolled oats into a large bowl, pour over the melted mix and stir to combine, then firmly press the mixture into the base of the tin. Bake for 20–25 minutes until it is starting to brown around the edges and firming up.

Leave to cool fully in the tin before cutting into squares.

MILLIONAIRE'S SHORTBREAD

Makes: 16

Prep: 20 minutes
Bake: 20–25 minutes
Set: 3 hours
Lasts: 1+ week, in a fridge or at room
temperature

SHORTBREAD:
100g caster sugar
200g unsalted butter
275g plain flour

CARAMEL:
200g unsalted butter
3 tbsp caster sugar
4 tbsp golden syrup
395g condensed milk

DECORATION:
200g milk chocolate
100g white chocolate

Caramel squares, millionaire's shortbread, homemade Twix bar... whatever you call these they are one of my favourite things on the planet. What's not to love about a homemade shortbread base, dreamy caramel and a chocolate topping? The shortbread has only three ingredients and is so simple. Making your own caramel can be daunting, but is so worth it as it will set perfectly and has the best texture.

Preheat the oven to 180°C/160°C fan and line a deep, 23cm square tin with parchment paper.

First make the shortbread. Cream together the sugar and butter in a stand mixer with the paddle attachment until smooth. Mix in the flour until a dough is formed. It will be crumbly but the ingredients will be evenly dispersed. Firmly press the mixture into the base of the lined tin and bake for 20–25 minutes until pale golden on top. Once baked, remove from the oven and set aside.

Put all the caramel ingredients into a large pan and melt over a medium heat until the sugar has dissolved. Stir frequently to stop it catching. Once the sugar has dissolved, turn the heat up to high, let the mixture come to the boil and boil for 5–7 minutes, stirring constantly so that the mixture does not catch on the bottom of the pan. BE CAREFUL as the mixture is VERY hot and can burn you if it splashes back. The mixture will be ready when it has changed to a slightly darker golden colour, and has thickened to a soft fudge texture. Pour the caramel onto the shortbread base and leave to set for 1 hour in the fridge.

Continued overleaf →

Once set, melt the chocolate for the topping. I add each chocolate to a separate heatproof bowl and melt in the microwave but you can also melt over a pan of simmering water (bain-marie). Pour the milk chocolate over the chilled caramel in an even layer, then pour the white chocolate in small amounts over the milk chocolate and swirl the two chocolates together with a skewer.

Chill the shortbread in the fridge for another 1–2 hours until the chocolate topping has hardened. Cut into 16 pieces and enjoy.

CUSTOMISE:
The shortbread can be flavoured – add the zest of 1 lemon or orange, or add 1 tsp of a flavouring, such as vanilla extract.

The caramel can also be flavoured in the same way – but personally I love it as it is.

I use a mixture of milk and white chocolate for the topping – but you can use any that you like! Dark, milk, white, flavoured, or you can even mix your chocolate of choice with a spread, such as a chocolate spread!

RHUBARB & CUSTARD BLONDIES

 Makes: 16

Prep: 45 minutes
Bake: 30–35 minutes
Cool: 2 hours
Lasts: 1+ week, at room temperature

175g rhubarb
300g white granulated sugar
2 tbsp water
200g unsalted butter, melted
3 eggs
125g plain flour
75g custard powder
200g white chocolate chips or chunks
100g custard

CUSTOMISE:

I use fresh or tinned rhubarb depending on the season – if using tinned rhubarb, use the syrup from the tin instead of the 2 tbsp water.

You can use ready-made custard, or make up some custard using more custard powder.

You can leave out the white chocolate chips or chunks or swap them for a different flavour chocolate.

The rhubarb can be swapped for another fruit such as cherries, blackberries, or even apples!

Rhubarb and custard is an iconic flavour combination – whether you think of those boiled sweets (my parents used to adore these) or even just stewed rhubarb topped with fresh custard, the sweet tang you get from the rhubarb, combined with the lovely flavour of custard, it really is amazing. Add these delicious flavours to a blondie traybake and it wins everyone's favourite bake!

Chop the rhubarb into pieces, and add to a pan with 50g of the sugar and the water. Place over a medium heat, stirring occasionally, for about 5 minutes, or until the rhubarb softens. Set aside to cool.

Preheat the oven to 180°C/160°C fan and line a 23cm square tin with parchment paper.

Put the melted unsalted butter and remaining 250g sugar into a large bowl and beat until smooth. Add the eggs and beat until smooth, then add the plain flour and custard powder and beat until combined. Fold through the white chocolate chips or chunks.

Pour the mixture into the tin and spread out evenly. Dollop the rhubarb mixture and custard over the top and swirl through slightly using a cake skewer or knife.

Bake the blondies for 30–35 minutes, or until there is an ever so slight wobble in the middle. Leave the blondies to cool fully in the tin before cutting into 16 squares.

Image overleaf →

BAKEWELL COOKIE BARS

♥ **Makes: 16**

Prep: 20 minutes
Bake: 18–22 minutes
Lasts: 1+ week, in a fridge or at room
temperature

225g plain flour
50g ground almonds
1 tsp bicarbonate of soda
115g unsalted butter, melted
55g white granulated sugar
135g soft light brown sugar
1 egg
½ tsp vanilla extract
1 tsp almond extract
200g white chocolate chips or chunks
100g glacé cherries, chopped

Just like my Bakewell Blondies, these are absolutely incredible if, like me, you adore the delicious almond flavour. This bake is slightly more cookie like, and just incredible. Cookie bars are basically cookies, but baked into a traybake, making them an easy bake.

Preheat the oven to 190°C/170°C fan and line a 23cm square tin with parchment paper.

Whisk the plain flour, ground almonds and bicarbonate of soda together in a bowl so all the ingredients are evenly distributed.

Add the melted butter and both sugars to another larger bowl and whisk for about 2 minutes so the sugars start to dissolve and the mixture is smooth. Add the egg, vanilla extract and almond extract and whisk again briefly until smooth.

Add the dry ingredients, the chocolate chips and chopped glacé cherries and mix with a spatula until a thick cookie dough is formed. Press the mixture into the base of the lined tin.

Bake for 18–22 minutes, then leave to cool fully in the tin before cutting into 16 bars. Enjoy!

CUSTOMISE:
The cookie bars can be made into cookies (without the jam): divide the dough into 15, roll into balls and bake on baking trays lined with parchment paper for about 10 minutes.

Sprinkle about 25g flaked almonds over the top before baking.

The white chocolate chips can be swapped to milk or dark chocolate.

MILLIONAIRE'S COOKIE BARS

Makes: 16

Prep: 20 minutes
Bake: 18–22 minutes
Set: 3 hours
Lasts: 1+ week, in a fridge or at room temperature

275g plain flour
1 tsp bicarbonate of soda
½ tsp sea salt
1 tbsp cornflour
115g unsalted butter, melted
55g white granulated sugar
135g soft light brown sugar
1 egg
1 tsp vanilla extract
100g white chocolate chips
100g milk chocolate chips
100g dark chocolate chips

CARAMEL:
200g unsalted butter
3 tbsp caster sugar
4 tbsp golden syrup
395g condensed milk

DECORATION:
100g white chocolate
100g milk chocolate
100g dark chocolate

This recipe really is heaven in a bar and is a firm favourite on my blog. Triple-chocolate-chip cookie bars topped with homemade caramel and a triple chocolate topping... Millionaire's Cookie Bars will be your new favourite bake! I went for a mix of white, milk and dark chocolate chips, as I just adore how it looks and tastes, but you can use all white, all milk, or all dark.

First make the cookie bars. Preheat the oven to 190°C/170°C fan and line a 23cm square tin with parchment paper.

Whisk the plain flour, bicarbonate of soda, sea salt and cornflour together in a bowl so all the ingredients are evenly distributed. Put the melted butter and both sugars in a separate larger bowl and whisk for about 2 minutes so the sugars start to dissolve and the mixture is smooth. Add the egg and the vanilla extract and whisk again briefly until smooth.

Add the dry ingredients and the chocolate chips and mix with a spatula until a thick cookie dough is formed. Press the mixture into the base of the lined tin, then bake for 18–22 minutes. Remove from the oven and leave to cool in the tin while you make the caramel.

Pour all the caramel ingredients into a large pan and melt over a medium heat until the sugar has dissolved, stirring frequently to stop anything from catching.

Once the sugar has dissolved, turn the heat up high, let the mixture come to the boil and bubble for 5–7 minutes, stirring constantly so that the mixture does not catch on the bottom of the pan. BE CAREFUL as the mixture is VERY hot and can burn you if it splashes back. The mixture will be ready when it has changed to a slightly darker golden colour, and has thickened to a soft fudge texture. Pour the caramel onto the cookie base and leave to set for 1 hour in the fridge.

Once the caramel has set, melt the three chocolates in separate heatproof bowls (either in a microwave or over a pan of simmering water). Randomly pour and spoon the chocolates over the set caramel, and swirl with a cake skewer to create a beautiful pattern. Return to the fridge for another 1–2 hours until the chocolate has hardened, then cut into 16 bars and enjoy.

NO-BAKE WHITE CHOCOLATE TIFFIN

♥ Makes: 16

Prep: 20 minutes
Set: 2 hours
Lasts: 1+ week, at room temperature
or in the fridge

400g white chocolate, finely chopped
50g unsalted butter
200g biscuits, chopped
100g glacé cherries
100g dried cranberries
25g desiccated coconut

TOPPING:
100g white chocolate, melted

CUSTOMISE:
You can swap the cranberries for
100g raisins.

I like to use digestives but you can
use any biscuit you like.

You can add extras to replace the
biscuits, cherries, cranberries or
coconut, such as:

- 50g mini marshmallows

- 100g large marshmallows

- 75g cereal (such as cornflakes,
  rice pops)

- 100g chocolate sweets

Tiffin and rocky road are extremely similar treats, but to me tiffin is something that is usually quite biscuit-based, with fruity additions such as raisins, sultanas, or in this case, dried cranberries. White chocolate and cranberries together are utterly scrumptious, and along with the biscuits, glacé cherries and desiccated coconut you have a wonderful no-bake white chocolate traybake of heaven.

Line a 20–23cm square tin with parchment paper and set aside.

Put the white chocolate and butter into a heatproof bowl and melt together until smooth. I do this in the microwave in short 10–15 second bursts but you could also set the bowl over a pan of simmering water (bain-marie).

Put the chopped biscuits, glacé cherries, dried cranberries and desiccated coconut into a separate bowl and stir until they are mixed well, then pour over the melted white chocolate mixture. Fold the mixture together until everything is covered in chocolate. Pour into the prepared tin and spread until it is even. Drizzle over the melted white chocolate for the topping and then chill in the fridge for 2 hours until set.

Cut into 16 pieces and enjoy!

NO-BAKE ROCKY ROAD

♥ Makes: 16

Prep: 20 minutes
Set: 2 hours
Lasts: 1+ week, at room temperature
or in the fridge

125g golden syrup
125g unsalted butter
250g milk chocolate, finely chopped
250g dark chocolate, finely chopped
100g mini marshmallows
200g digestive biscuits, chopped
200g chocolates

Rocky road is an easy, no-bake chocolatey traybake that is full of your favourite things. I make mine with a base of milk chocolate, dark chocolate, unsalted butter and golden syrup but you can, of course, just use chocolate if you want – simply melt some chocolate, mix in your favourite treats, and set it in the fridge! I, however, simply love the flavour of syrup and butter. My favourite basic rocky road uses mini marshmallows, chopped up digestive biscuits and some random chocolates. The absolute best!

Line a 20–23cm square tin with parchment paper and set aside.

Put the golden syrup and butter into a large pan and melt over a low heat until combined and smooth. Take the pan off the heat, add the chopped chocolate and stir the mixture together until smooth. Once it's melted and combined, leave to cool for a couple of minutes.

Put the mini marshmallows, chopped digestive biscuits and chocolates into a large bowl and mix briefly. Pour over the melted chocolate mix and fold together. Pour into the tin and spread until it is even. Refrigerate for about 2 hours until set, then cut into 16 pieces.

CHANGE UP THE BASE:
You can use all milk chocolate in the base but I would increase the quantity to 600g total.

You can also use all dark chocolate in the base but I would decrease the quantity to 400g total.

You can use a base of just melted chocolate instead of using syrup and butter. Use 600g melted chocolate in total.

CUSTOMISE:
As this is a no-bake treat, you can basically add what you want. I use mini marshmallows, chopped digestive biscuits and chocolates but you can add any of the following (generally stick to a maximum of 500g added extras):

· 100g glace cherries

· 200g any chopped biscuits

· 150g dried fruit (such as raisins, currants, sultanas)

· 100g large marshmallows

· 75g cereal (such as cornflakes, rice pops)

NO-BAKE MINT SLICE

Serves: 16

Prep: 30 minutes
Set: 3 hours
Lasts: 1+ week, in the fridge

BISCUIT BASE:
400g digestive biscuits
150g unsalted butter, melted
100g condensed milk

MINT FILLING:
350g icing sugar
2 tsp peppermint extract
½ tsp green food colouring
2–3 tbsp water

TOPPING:
300g milk chocolate, melted

This has always been one of my favourite things to eat for as long as I can remember. We had it every now and again at my junior school for pudding and I loved it so much – I set out to recreate the delicious biscuity, minty, chocolatey, scrumptious dessert that made me obsessed with baking and it's pretty popular on my blog too.

Line a 23cm square tin with parchment paper and set aside.

Crush the digestive biscuits to a fine crumb in a food processor, or bash in a bowl with the end of a rolling pin. Mix in the melted butter and condensed milk until combined. Press the mixture into the base of the tin and chill while you make the filling.

Mix the icing sugar, peppermint extract and food colouring together, then add ½ tablespoon of water at a time, mixing well all the time, until you have a thick paste. Spread this across the biscuit base and leave to set in the fridge for 1 hour.

Melt the milk chocolate for the topping in a heatproof bowl (either in the microwave or set over a pan of simmering water). Pour this on top of the filling and carefully spread over the traybake, trying not to disturb the filling too much. Return to the fridge to set for 1–2 hours, or until the chocolate has set.

Cut the mint slice into 16 pieces and enjoy!

CUSTOMISE:

The condensed milk in the base can be replaced with 50g more unsalted butter.

The green food colouring is optional – it is just to make it look mint flavoured!

The mint flavouring can be swapped for a different flavour, such as lemon, orange or coffee.

Adding 1–2 tbsp vegetable/sunflower oil to the melted chocolate topping can make the traybake easier to cut.

SALTED CARAMEL PRETZEL SLICE

♥ Makes: 16

Prep: 45 minutes
Bake: 20–25 minutes
Set: 3 hours
Lasts: 1+ week, in a fridge or at room temperature

BASE:
100g caster sugar
200g unsalted butter
275g plain flour
Pinch of salt
50g salted pretzels

CARAMEL:
250g white granulated sugar
75ml water
60g unsalted butter
200ml double cream
1 tsp vanilla extract
½ tsp sea salt

DECORATION:
50g milk or dark chocolate, melted
50g salted pretzels

CUSTOMISE:
If you want a firmer set caramel, you can use the caramel from my Millionaire's Shortbread (see page 141).

If you want to cover the caramel completely with melted chocolate instead of drizzling, use 250g melted chocolate and pour over evenly.

When I think of snacking on something simple but salty, I always think of pretzels. I know typically people would think of crisps, but I just loooove a pretzel. Combining sweet and salty by putting together salted caramel sauce and pretzels is the absolute dream! A shortbread base, pretzels, salted caramel topping and more... what could be better?

Preheat the oven to 180°C/160°C fan and line a deep, 23cm square tin with parchment paper.

First make the base. Cream together the sugar and butter in a stand mixer with the paddle attachment until smooth. Mix in the flour and salt until a dough is formed. It will be crumbly but the ingredients will be evenly dispersed. Firmly press the mixture into the base of the tin and press the pretzels on top. Bake for 20–25 minutes until pale golden on top. Remove from the oven and set aside while you make the caramel.

Put the sugar and water into a large pan and place over a low heat until the sugar has dissolved. Once the sugar has dissolved, turn the heat up and stop stirring. Wait for the mixture to boil to an amber colour (this can take 5–10 minutes).

Take the mixture off the heat, add the butter and stir until it has melted. Slowly pour in the cream, stirring all the time, then bring the mixture back to the boil and bubble for at least a minute. Remove from the heat, add the vanilla and sea salt and whisk until smooth, then pour the caramel onto the base and leave to set for 1 hour in the fridge.

Once the caramel has set, drizzle the melted chocolate over the top, and add the pretzels. Return to the fridge to set again until the chocolate is firm. Divide into 16 portions and enjoy!

Desserts

Desserts are part of the fun when it comes to having dinner, whether it's with your friends or family, your other half, at a social occasion, or even at a full-on wedding. Everyone loves dessert – I always find that even after a dinner when I feel like I am full to burst, I can still fit in something sweet afterwards.

I adore savoury food, I love having a starter and really delicious meal, but a dessert afterwards just finishes it off and is absolutely heavenly. Whether you go down the route of puddings, pies, tarts, or ice cream, making delicious, indulgent desserts is one of the best things about baking.

In this chapter you will find desserts that are sure to please anyone, or you can customise them to make your own versions too. I've included some blog favourites like my Caramel Apple Crumble Pie and Billionaire's Tart but there are plenty of new recipes to enjoy as well. You'll find comforting recipes for chilly winter evenings, like sticky toffee pudding, and others that are perfect for those hot summer days when turning the oven on is the last thing you want to do.

The other wonderful thing about desserts is that they are so easy to customise – whether that's how you want to serve your dessert (with ice cream, custard or cream, for example) or whether you want to switch the ingredients, for example turning a white chocolate and raspberry tart into a blackberry tart. Anything is possible!

MY TOP TIPS FOR DESSERTS:

1 Don't be tempted to substitute the ingredients for lower fat alternatives! You'll run the risk of changing the texture or just not getting the results you are after – fat content is so important in baking and it will create the best dessert ever!

2 If a dessert needs time to set in the fridge, don't skip it! It will help create your perfect dessert that you can enjoy with your friends and family.

3 Use the correct size dish – whether it is for a no-bake dessert, or a baked one – this is always important.

PAVLOVA

Prep: 30 minutes
Bake: 1 hour
Cool: 3 hours
Lasts: 1–2 days, in the fridge

5 large egg whites
300g caster sugar
1 tsp white wine vinegar
1 tsp cornflour
1 tsp vanilla extract

DECORATION:
450ml double cream
2 tbsp icing sugar
1 tsp vanilla extract
400g berries (such as strawberries, blackberries, raspberries, blueberries, cherries)
Fresh mint leaves

CUSTOMISE:
The vinegar and cornflour are optional, but create a lovely texture.

You can use any berry, or any other type of fruit you want for the topping, such as kiwi fruit, nectarines or peaches.

You can fold 40g cocoa powder through the meringue to make a chocolate meringue.

Swirling 50ml fruit coulis through the whipped cream creates a wonderful flavour and it looks pretty too!

Meringue is light, airy, and something I always have room for – even after a full dinner. I adore Eton Mess, meringues topped with chocolate, meringues on their own... but what I really love is pavlova. Crisp on the outside, soft and marshmallowy inside, topped with sweetened cream and your favourite fruits – it's easy to make, and always looks so impressive!

Preheat the oven to 150°C/130°C fan and line a large baking tray with parchment paper.

Whisk the egg whites with an electric hand whisk until the mixture forms stiff peaks. You want to lift your whisk out of the egg whites, and for them to hold their shape.

Still whisking, start adding the sugar, 1 teaspoon at a time. Once all of the caster sugar is incorporated, it should look smooth and glossy. Whisk in the white wine vinegar, then the cornflour, then the vanilla extract and whisk until smooth.

Using a small dab of meringue in each corner, stick your parchment paper to the tray. Spoon the meringue onto the tray, creating a circle that is about 25cm in diameter. You can make it smaller and taller, or larger and shorter – just make sure it fits on the baking tray.

Bake the pavlova for 1 hour. Once baked, turn the oven off and leave the pavlova to fully cool in the oven, without opening the door, for about 3 hours.

When you are ready to serve, whip the double cream with the icing sugar and vanilla extract to soft peaks. Lightly dollop the cream on top of the meringue and add the berries on top (make sure you wash them thoroughly first). Finish with a few sprigs of mint and serve.

INDIVIDUAL STICKY TOFFEE PUDDINGS

♥ Makes: 8

Prep: 45 minutes
Bake: 20–25 minutes
Cool: 15 minutes
Lasts: 2–3 days, in the fridge

175g pitted dates, chopped
175ml boiling water
75g unsalted butter
175g soft dark brown sugar
3 eggs
250g self-raising flour
1 tsp baking powder
1 tsp bicarbonate of soda
75g black treacle
100ml full-fat milk

SAUCE:
75g unsalted butter
75g soft dark brown sugar
2 tbsp black treacle
1 tsp vanilla extract
225ml double cream

SERVING IDEAS:
Double cream
Vanilla ice cream
Whipped cream

CUSTOMISE:
You can use golden syrup as an alternative to black treacle.

These puddings can be baked in a large dish instead of individual ones for 40 minutes.

When I think of pudding I think of something warm, cosy and delicious. A baked pudding with a delicious warm sauce or topping is the dream – and sticky toffee pudding hits the spot every time. This is one of those puddings that is on nearly every single pub menu all year round – it's a classic that you can't beat. However, making it at home means you can enjoy it whenever and however you like. I serve mine with a giant scoop of ice cream, and some extra sauce.

Put the chopped dates into a bowl and pour over the boiling water. Set aside for 20 minutes.

Preheat the oven to 180°C/160°C fan and grease and flour 8 pudding moulds.

Put the butter, sugar, eggs, flour, baking powder, bicarbonate of soda and treacle into a bowl and beat until combined, taking care not to overmix. Add the chopped dates and water, and then the milk a little at a time. Mix until smooth (it will be a thin mixture).

Divide the mixture between the pudding moulds and bake for 20–25 minutes, or until a skewer inserted in the middle comes out clean. Leave the puddings to cool for about 15 minutes while you make the sauce.

Put all of the sauce ingredients into a large pan, place over a low-medium heat and stir until the sugar has dissolved and the butter has melted. Bring the sauce to the boil and stir for 1–2 minutes so it thickens slightly.

Carefully remove the puddings from their moulds and then pour the sauce over them. Serve with a drizzle of cream, whipped cream, or ice cream.

TRIPLE CHOCOLATE COOKIE DOUGH DESSERTS

Serves: 2

Prep: 10 minutes
Bake: 12–15 minutes
Cool: 10 minutes
Lasts: 2–3 days (but best served fresh)

60g unsalted butter, melted
100g soft light brown sugar
1 egg (small or medium)
½ tsp vanilla extract
100g plain flour
25g cocoa powder
Pinch of bicarbonate of soda
50g white chocolate chips
50g milk chocolate chips
50g dark chocolate chips
Vanilla ice cream, to serve

CUSTOMISE:

These are best served warm – but you can reheat them in the oven or microwave.

You can make these plain by replacing the cocoa powder with another 25g plain flour.

You can use any type of chocolate in your cookie dough – I just love triple chocolate! Stick to 150g in total.

You can flavour the cookie dough with ½ tsp orange extract or peppermint extract.

Well, let's just start this by saying that I LOVE COOKIES. They are one of my favourite treats, possibly beating cheesecakes (I know, that's a bit of a shocker). What I love about cookies is that you can bake a classic cookie, or cookie bars, or make indulgent desserts like this firm favourite on my blog – gooey, delicious cookie dough served with ice cream and oodles of chocolate.

Preheat the oven to 180°C/160°C fan and get 2 dishes ready. I use 12cm wide crème brûlée dishes, but anything similar will work.

Pour the melted butter into a bowl and add the sugar. Whisk together until the sugar has dissolved slightly. Add the egg and vanilla extract and mix well again.

Add the flour, cocoa powder, bicarbonate of soda and chocolate chips and mix well until it comes together to form a lovely thick cookie dough. Divide the mixture equally between the dishes and bake for 12–15 minutes, or until dry on top and just cooked through in the middle – the gooier the better!

Remove from the oven and let them cool for about 10 minutes and then serve with a giant dollop of ice cream.

LEMON POSSET TART

Serves: 10–12

Prep: 30 minutes
Set: 4 hours
Lasts: 3 days, in the fridge

BISCUIT CRUST:
300g digestive biscuits
150g unsalted butter, melted

LEMON POSSET FILLING:
600ml double cream
200g caster sugar
Zest of 3 lemons
85ml lemon juice (about 2 lemons)

DECORATION:
150ml double cream
2 tbsp icing sugar
5g freeze-dried raspberries
Biscuit crumbs

CUSTOMISE:
The filling can be used to make 12 individual lemon possets – simply pour into 12 ramekins or small glasses and leave to set.

You can use different citrus flavours such as orange or lime – use the zest of 2 large oranges or 4 limes, and the same amount of juice.

You can add some raspberries to the mix, or some other berries if you want to add another texture to this no-bake dessert.

I have always adored lemon posset – who knew that combining sugar, cream and lemon could lead to something SO good? This favourite from my blog is a very simple dessert to make – all you do is mix cream and sugar together, heat and then add the lemon zest and juice. The tart base here is a classic cheesecake base of digestive biscuits mixed with melted butter.

Blitz the digestive biscuits in a food processor to a fine crumb or bash them in a bowl with a rolling pin. Add the melted butter and mix together until combined. Spread onto the base and sides of a 23cm loose-bottomed tart tin. I usually start on the sides, and then cover the bottom last to make sure it's a secure biscuit case. Set aside while you make the filling.

Pour the double cream and caster sugar into a large pan and heat gently over a low heat, stirring until the sugar has dissolved. Turn the heat up to medium and heat the mixture until it starts to boil gently, stir frequently to stop the mixture from catching on the bottom. Let it simmer for 1 minute and then turn off the heat.

Stir in the lemon zest and juice and then pour onto the biscuit base – refrigerate for at least 4 hours, or preferably overnight so it has time to set properly.

When you are ready to serve, whisk together the double cream and icing sugar until you have soft peaks. Pipe the cream onto your tart, then sprinkle on some freeze-dried raspberries and some biscuit crumbs to decorate.

BILLIONAIRE'S TART

Serves: 10–12

Prep: 30 minutes
Set: 4 hours
Lasts: 3 days, in the fridge

BISCUIT CRUST:
300g digestive biscuits
2 tbsp cocoa powder
150g unsalted butter, melted

FILLING:
250g dulce de leche
Pinch of sea salt
300ml double cream
125g dark chocolate, chopped
125g milk chocolate, chopped
50g unsalted butter

DECORATION:
Miniature shortbread bites
Sprinkles

CUSTOMISE:
You can use a plain biscuit base by removing the cocoa powder.

The sea salt is optional if you don't like salted caramel, but you can also swap the caramel to any chocolate spread, or even your favourite jam!

If you would like to use all dark chocolate, use 250g. If you would like to use all milk chocolate, use 350g.

Yes that's right… Billionaire's Tart. Honestly, I'm in love with this recipe. I decided to call it a Billionaire's Tart rather than a Millionaire's Tart because it has a chocolate crust rather than a plain one, plus a salted caramel filling, a chocolate ganache topping and shortbread bites on top! This no-bake recipe is a favourite on my blog where it includes plenty of customisable hints on using homemade pastry, or even making your own caramel sauce.

Blitz the digestive biscuits to a fine crumb in a food processor or bash the biscuits in a bowl with a rolling pin. Add the cocoa powder, and mix again briefly. Add the melted butter and mix together until combined. Spread onto the base and sides of a 23cm loose-bottomed tart tin. I usually start on the sides, and then cover the bottom last to make sure it's a secure biscuit case.

Spread the dulce de leche over the biscuit base, and sprinkle on some sea salt.

Heat the cream to just before boiling point. Meanwhile, put the dark and milk chocolate and butter into a separate bowl. Pour the hot cream into the bowl and whisk together until smooth. If there are any chunks of chocolate left, microwave the mixture in 10-second bursts, stirring each time, or return the mixture to your pan briefly to melt. Carefully pour the chocolate mixture over the caramel and refrigerate for 1 hour.

Remove the tart from the fridge and decorate with the shortbread bites and some sprinkles. Return to the fridge to set for a further 3 hours.

WHITE CHOCOLATE & RASPBERRY TART

Serves: 8–10

Prep: 1 hour
Bake: 30 minutes
Set: 2 hours
Lasts: 3 days, in the fridge

BISCUIT CRUST:
300g digestive biscuits
150g unsalted butter, melted

RASPBERRY COULIS:
100g raspberries
1 tbsp caster sugar
2 tbsp water

WHITE CHOCOLATE FILLING:
600g white chocolate, broken
  into pieces
25g unsalted butter
250ml double cream

DECORATION:
100g fresh raspberries
5g freeze-dried raspberries

Every year I go fruit picking at a local farm, as nothing can beat a freshly grown piece of fruit at the peak of the season. Usually it's strawberries, but these days I often end up with an abundance of raspberries and naturally that classic combination of white chocolate and raspberry screamed out to me again! We all know I am completely obsessed with it (and from the reactions to this recipe on the blog it seems you are too) but I just can't stop! This no-bake dessert is indulgent, sweet and rich – and the perfect dinner party dessert.

BISCUIT CRUST:
Blitz the digestive biscuits in a food processor to a fine crumb or bash the biscuits in a bowl with a rolling pin. Add the melted butter and mix together until combined. Spread onto the base and sides of an 23cm loose-bottomed tart tin. I usually start on the sides, and then cover the bottom last to make sure it's a secure biscuit case. Set aside while you make the coulis and filling.

RASPBERRY COULIS:
Put the raspberries, sugar and water into a pan and place over a low-medium heat until the fruit starts to break down and soften. After 3–4 minutes, remove from the heat and use a hand-held blender to purée to a liquid. Pass the coulis through a sieve to remove the seeds and let the mixture cool.

Continued overleaf →

WHITE CHOCOLATE & RASPBERRY TART
CONTINUED

CUSTOMISE:
If you want to use milk chocolate, use a ratio of 400g milk chocolate and 200ml double cream.

If you want to use dark chocolate, use a ratio of 300g dark chocolate and 300ml double cream.

The fruit coulis can be made with other berries, or a combination. The process is the same, as long as you use 100g prepared fruit.

WHITE CHOCOLATE FILLING:
Put the white chocolate and butter into a large bowl. Pour the cream into a small pan and heat until just before it starts to boil. Pour onto the chocolate and butter and leave to sit for 5 minutes, then whisk the mixture until it is smooth and combined. If any lumps of chocolate remain, return the mixture back to the pan and heat over a low heat until smooth.

Pour the filling into the tart case, dollop in half of the raspberry coulis and swirl the mixture together. Chill the tart in the fridge for a couple of hours until set.

DECORATION:
When you are ready to serve, decorate the tart with some fresh and freeze-dried raspberries and serve with the remaining coulis.

MILLIONAIRE'S TRIFLE

♥ Serves: 12+

Prep: 45 minutes
Set: 1 hour
Lasts: 2–3 days, in the fridge

500ml ready-made vanilla custard
100g ready-made caramel
100g milk or dark chocolate,
   chopped
600ml double cream
2 tbsp icing sugar
1 tsp vanilla extract
1 x jumbo chocolate Swiss roll
500g shortbread biscuits
300g caramel sauce

TOPPING:
1 x packet brownie bites
100g chocolate sauce
Chocolates
Sprinkles

CUSTOMISE:

You can use chocolate sponge, or any type of cake in place of the Swiss roll. You can also use a vanilla sponge as well.

You can add 1–2 tsp sea salt to the caramel to make salted caramel.

You can swap the caramel for chocolate sauce, or a fruit coulis.

You can add a layer of jelly if you want – follow the instructions on the packet.

Typically, a trifle has the classic flavours of sponge cake, fruit, custard, jelly and cream. There is nothing wrong with regular trifle... but Millionaire's Trifle? Oh my, it is heaven. Chocolate custard, caramel, chocolate Swiss roll, brownies, cream and more! It sounds a bit OTT, but it is secretly everyone's dream in a bite. It's fun to make, always a crowd-pleaser, and I promise you will love it as much as I do.

Pour the ready-made custard into a pan, add the caramel and chocolate and heat over a low heat, mixing together until smooth and melted. Pour into a bowl and leave to cool, stirring occasionally to prevent a skin forming.

Put the double cream, icing sugar and vanilla extract into a separate bowl and whip together to form soft peaks.

Slice the Swiss roll into 1cm round slices and then place a layer of slices into the bottom of a large serving dish about 20cm in diameter and 10cm deep (glass is best so you can see the layers). Add half of the custard mixture and spread evenly, then add a layer of shortbread biscuits. Add a third of the whipped cream and then drizzle over a third of the caramel sauce.

Repeat with another layer of Swiss roll slices, the other half of the custard, another layer of shortbread biscuits, a third of the whipped cream and a third of the caramel sauce.

Top with a layer of brownie bites and the remaining whipped cream. Drizzle over some chocolate sauce, the rest of the caramel sauce and any decoration you fancy, such as sprinkles, or chocolates!

Leave the trifle in the fridge to set for about 1 hour before tucking in.

CHOCOLATE MOUSSE

 Makes: 6–8 small mousses

Prep: 40 minutes
Set: 3–4 hours
Lasts: 2 days, in the fridge

150g dark chocolate
25g unsalted butter
3 eggs, separated
30g caster sugar
150ml double cream

Chocolate mousse is something that I have always enjoyed – shop-bought, in a restaurant, but especially homemade. I find making chocolate mousse so satisfying as seeing the mixture transform from five simple ingredients is amazing. This chocolate mousse is rich and decadent. It can be made in one large serving dish, shot glasses, or in small glasses to make individual portions.

Put the chocolate into a heatproof bowl with the butter. Melt in the microwave until smooth. Alternatively, set the bowl over a pan of simmering water (bain-marie) and stir until melted. Leave the chocolate mixture to cool for 10 minutes.

Put the egg yolks into a bowl with the caster sugar and whisk together until they are light in colour, pale and thick. Pour the cooled chocolate and butter mixture into the egg yolk mixture and stir together.

Meanwhile, use an electric hand whisk to whisk the egg whites to stiff peaks. Carefully fold the whipped egg whites into the chocolate mixture, being careful not to knock out all the air. Spoon the mixture into serving glasses, and then chill in the fridge for 3–4 hours before enjoying.

CUSTOMISE:
The best chocolate to use for this is 70% dark chocolate. If you prefer milk chocolate, you will need to increase the amount to 225g.

You can decorate the mousse with 150ml cream whipped with 2 tbsp icing sugar.

Fresh fruit such as strawberries and raspberries are the best fresh decoration for these mousses.

CARAMEL APPLE CRUMBLE PIE

Serves: 12

Prep: 1 hour
Bake: 45–55 minutes
Cool: 30 minutes
Lasts: 2–3 days, in the fridge (but best served fresh)

PASTRY BASE:

175g plain flour
1 tbsp icing sugar
100g chilled unsalted butter, diced
1 egg yolk
1 tbsp cold water

PIE FILLING:

500g peeled and cored cooking
   apples
100g soft light brown sugar
½ tsp ground cinnamon
2 tbsp water
100g caramel

CRUMBLE MIX:

120g plain flour
60g caster sugar
60g chilled unsalted butter, diced

Vanilla or clotted cream ice cream,
   to serve

Caramel flavours, apple crumble, and pastry… can you think of anything more warming, cosy and utterly delicious on a cold day? Every time I post about this one on my blog I always get such a good reaction because it is the epitome of cosy in a dessert. The pastry makes a crunchy base for the pie as it is blind baked (no soggy bottoms here!), the apple crumble filling is a classic that everyone knows, but topped with caramel it is even more indulgent. The crumble topping is something that I just cannot resist!

Put all the pastry ingredients into a food processor and blitz quickly on the pulse setting until the mixture starts to bind – it shouldn't take too long at all! If you don't have a food processor, add the ingredients to a large bowl and rub with your fingertips until it resembles breadcrumbs. Then, bring the mixture together with your hands.

Grease and flour a deep, 23cm loose-bottomed tart tin. Roll out the pastry on a lightly floured work surface to the thickness of a pound coin. Press the pastry into the tin and trim and neaten the edges. Fill any gaps with any excess pastry so the tin is completely covered, then chill in the fridge for 30 minutes.

Meanwhile, preheat the oven to 200°C/180°C fan. Cover the pastry with a piece of parchment paper and fill with baking beans or rice. Bake the pastry 'blind' for 15 minutes, then remove the beans and parchment and return to the oven to bake for a further 5–10 minutes, or until the pastry is cooked through and turning golden. Leave to cool in the tin while you make the filling.

Continued overleaf →

CUSTOMISE:

The apples can be swapped for other crumble fruits, such as blackberries, cherries, or even a mixture! You just want the fruit to be the same weight.

Shop-bought shortcrust pastry works perfectly if you don't want to make your own – you can just blind bake it and then fill as described in the recipe.

If you want to change the fruit, you may also want to leave out the caramel – it's up to you!

When baking with apples, I recommend a cooking apple such as Bramley.

Chop the apples into 3cm pieces, then add to a large heavy-based pan, along with the sugar, cinnamon and water. Cook over a medium heat, stirring, for 5 minutes, then cover with a lid, reduce the heat and leave to simmer for another 5 minutes. You basically need the fruit to still have texture and firmness. If the apples are getting soft very quickly, remove from the heat – you don't want them to be too liquid!

Make the crumble mix by rubbing together all the ingredients until the mixture resembles breadcrumbs.

Add the apple to the pastry case and carefully dollop over the caramel in small spoonfuls. Sprinkle over the crumble mixture and bake the pie for 25–30 minutes until the crumble mixture is golden on top. Remove from the oven and leave the pie to cool for about 30 minutes as it will be very hot. Once cooled slightly, remove from the tin and serve warm with a scoop of vanilla or clotted cream ice cream. Or you could leave it to cool completely and enjoy cold!

KEY LIME PIE

Serves: 12

Prep: 45 minutes
Bake: 12–15 minutes
Cool: 6+ hours
Lasts: 2–3 days, in the fridge

BASE:
300g digestive biscuits
150g unsalted butter, melted

FILLING:
3 egg yolks
780g condensed milk
Zest and juice of 5 limes

DECORATION:
150ml double cream
2 tbsp icing sugar
1 lime, thinly sliced

CUSTOMISE:
Try making this with a ginger nut base! Use 300g ginger nuts, but reduce the amount of melted butter to 100g.

Just like the Lemon Posset Tart (see page 163), you can also swap the lime for other citrus fruits such as orange, or lemon.

Key limes are very hard to find in the UK, so using a regular lime is absolutely fine.

I am an avid fan of no-bake treats, but when trying out this recipe I tested several versions, both no-bake and baked, but the baked was definitely the best. You can easily make a no-bake version by following the Lemon Posset Tart recipe on page 163 and swapping lemon for lime, but the creamier filling used here works so well with the lime flavour. I give you the perfect Key Lime Pie!

Blitz the digestive biscuits to a fine crumb in a food processor, or bash in a bowl with a rolling pin. Add the melted butter and mix until combined. Press into the sides and base of a 23cm loose-bottomed tart tin (mine was 3cm deep). Preheat the oven to 190°C/170°C fan.

Whisk the egg yolks in a large bowl until light and smooth, then add the condensed milk and whisk again until smooth. Add the lime zest and juice and briefly whisk again.

Pour the filling into the tart case and bake for 12–15 minutes, or until there is just a slight wobble in the middle. Leave to cool completely and then chill in the fridge overnight to set fully.

When you are ready to serve, whip the double cream with the icing sugar to soft peaks. Transfer to a piping bag and use to decorate the top of the pie. Finish with thin slices of lime.

NO-CHURN CHOCOLATE ICE CREAM

Serves: 10

Prep: 25 minutes
Freeze: 6+ hours
Lasts: 3 months, in the freezer

600ml double cream
397g tin condensed milk
50g cocoa powder
1 tsp vanilla extract
100g white/milk/dark chocolate, grated

CUSTOMISE:

Without freezing, this recipe will make mousse that you can pour into glasses and set in the fridge for a few hours.

Try the following flavour ideas:

- Add 275g cherry pie filling or cherries soaked in kirsch for a Black Forest ice cream.

- Add swirls of 275g caramel sauce for a chocolate caramel ice cream.

- Use 1 tsp peppermint extract for a mint chocolate ice cream.

- Use 1 tsp orange extract for a chocolate orange ice cream.

- Chop up 200g chocolate chip cookies and fold through for a cookie ice cream.

Ice cream can be something to enjoyed on its own – whether it's peak summer or whether you are just craving something sweet and quick – or it can be enjoyed on the side of a different dessert. There are two methods for making ice cream: a classic custard base that you would typically churn in an ice-cream machine, or the no-churn method as used here. Just two simple ingredients (double cream and condensed milk) create the base, to which you can add other flavours. Simply whip, freeze and enjoy!

Pour the double cream and condensed milk into a bowl and add the cocoa powder and vanilla extract. Whisk the mixture until it's an even colour and starts to thicken.

Fold through the grated chocolate, then pour the mixture into a container – I use a 900g loaf tin.

Freeze for at least 5–6 hours, or preferably overnight so it has time to get to the correct texture. Remove from the freezer about 20 minutes before serving to allow it to soften slightly.

NO-CHURN CHERRY BAKEWELL ICE CREAM

❤ **Serves: 10**

Prep: 25 minutes
Freeze: 6+ hours
Lasts: 3 months, in the freezer

200g pitted cherries
450ml double cream
397g tin condensed milk
1 tsp almond extract
½ tsp pink food colouring (optional)
Cherries and toasted flaked almonds,
   to serve

CUSTOMISE:
You can use an ice-cream machine to create the ice cream – just pour the mix into the machine and follow your machine's instructions.

The cherries can be swapped for cherry pie filling and blended in the same way.

You can swap the cherries for another fruit, such as strawberries, raspberries or blackberries.

The almond extract can left out or swapped for vanilla extract.

When you marry together almonds and cherries you get Cherry Bakewell. And with just blended cherries, double cream, condensed milk and almond extract you can create cherry bakewell ice cream! I like to add a smidge of pink food colouring to make it even prettier. A sprinkle of toasted almonds on top and some fresh cherries will give you a taste of heaven!

Add the pitted cherries to a blender and blitz until smooth. Pass through a sieve to remove any lumps and set aside.

Pour the double cream into a bowl and whip to stiff peaks.

Put the condensed milk, almond extract, pink food colouring (if using) and puréed cherries into a separate bowl and stir to combine. Fold through the whipped cream until combined, then pour the mixture into a container – I use a 900g loaf tin.

Freeze for at least 5–6 hours, or preferably overnight so it has time to get to the correct texture. Remove from the freezer about 20 minutes before serving to allow it to soften slightly. Scoop into bowls and serve topped with fresh cherries and toasted flaked almonds.

Image overleaf →

When it comes to wanting little treats or sweet things when baking, this chapter will definitely deliver, whether you are in the mood for scones, macarons, mug cakes or something deliciously chocolatey.

These bakes are perfect for tea time, that period in the afternoon when you want a sweet snack, although they can be used for any time of day. For example, the chocolate twists are amazing for breakfast, but are also a delicious evening treat and you can whip up a mug cake any time of the day (or night!). Generally though, the middle of the afternoon slump is the best time to enjoy any of these bakes.

Any classic afternoon tea menu, along with mini sandwiches, dainty cakes and tea in china cups, will include scones and macarons. In my opinion, you can't have a tea time chapter without either of these. Macarons have become almost iconic these days with people considering them elite afternoon treats and I would have to agree. They are much easier to make than you think and are perfect for decorating cakes, as part of a dessert, or just as they are. The options for flavouring and colouring your macarons are endless. Scones are also one of my favourite tea time treats. Plain scones topped with clotted cream and jam, or even fruity scones, or chocolate ones! Finally, you get into the other delicious tea time treats... mug cakes, microwaveable cookies, chocolate twists and cheesecake crêpes. All some of my favourite bakes that I know you guys will love too!

MY TOP TIPS FOR TEA TIME:

1 As this chapter covers a variety of techniques, it's important to think of the basics. Measure your ingredients accurately, as this will always give good results.

2 For scones, make sure not to overmix the dough. You want to bring the ingredients together as quickly and as simply as you can so you get the softest and most beautiful scones.

3 For macarons, don't be scared of failures! These are one of the hardest things to bake but they are so worth it. Make sure to follow all steps of the recipe as accurately as possible.

SCONES

Makes: 8

Prep: 20 minutes
Bake: 10–12 minutes
Cool: 20 minutes
Lasts: 2–3 days, at room temperature

350g self-raising flour, plus extra
   for dusting
100g chilled unsalted butter, cubed
1 tsp baking powder
Pinch of salt
50g caster sugar
200ml buttermilk
1 tsp vanilla extract
1 egg, beaten, for glazing

CUSTOMISE:
You can make your own buttermilk
by mixing 200ml full-fat milk with
2 tbsp lemon juice.

You can lightly flavour the scone
dough with the zest of 1 large
orange or 1 lemon, or 2 limes.

Make smaller scones with a 2–3cm
cutter and bake for 8–9 minutes
for a more bite-sized treat.

You can make them larger if you
prefer with a 6cm cutter – bake
for 14–15 minutes.

You can add 100g sultanas or
raisins to the dough after you have
added the buttermilk and vanilla
extract.

Scones are one of those things that I always crave and want all of a sudden, especially in the middle of the afternoon. It fits, as usually they are served for afternoon tea, with clotted cream and jam. Whether you put jam first or cream first, they are utterly delicious and are a firm favourite on my blog. There are so many variations of scones, but this classic version is just delightful!

Preheat the oven to 220°C/200°C fan and place a baking tray lined with parchment paper into the oven to preheat.

Tip the self-raising flour, butter, baking powder and salt into a food processor and pulse until the mixture resembles breadcrumbs. Alternatively, you can rub the mixture together with your fingertips to get the breadcrumb texture.

Pour the mixture into a large bowl and stir in the caster sugar. Add the buttermilk and vanilla extract, stir to combine and then knead slightly to bring together.

Sprinkle some extra flour onto a work surface and turn the dough out onto it. Gently roll it out, or press it down until it is about 4cm thick. Using a 5cm cutter, cut out the scones – you will have to re-roll the mixture a couple of times to get them all out of the mix.

Take the tray out of the oven, and arrange the scones on it. Brush the top of the scones with the beaten egg and bake for 10–12 minutes. Leave to cool for about 20 minutes before enjoying warm.

CHOCOLATE CHIP SCONES

♥ Makes: 10

Prep: 20 minutes
Bake: 10–12 minutes
Cool: 20 minutes
Lasts: 2–3 days, at room temperature

300g self-raising flour, plus extra
  for dusting
25g cocoa powder
125g chilled unsalted butter, cubed
2 tsp baking powder
Pinch of salt
50g caster sugar
200ml buttermilk
1 tsp vanilla extract
175g chocolate chips
1 egg, beaten, for glazing

FILLING & TOPPING:
75g milk chocolate, melted
Clotted cream
Chocolate spread

CUSTOMISE:
You can make your own buttermilk
by mixing 200ml full-fat milk with
2 tbsp lemon juice.

You can use whatever flavour
chocolate chips you like.

You can make the scones
chocolate orange flavoured by
adding the zest of 1 large orange.

You can make them mint chocolate
flavoured by adding 1 tsp
peppermint extract.

Rich and fudgy chocolate scones full of chocolate chips and with a chocolate drizzle on top, these are best served with clotted cream or whipped double cream, and your favourite chocolate spread! You can make them even more special by serving with fresh berries, such as strawberries or raspberries.

Preheat the oven to 220°C/200°C fan and place a baking tray lined with parchment paper into the oven to preheat.

Tip the self-raising flour, cocoa powder, butter, baking powder and salt into a food processor and pulse until the mixture resembles breadcrumbs. Alternatively, you can rub the mixture together with your fingertips to get the breadcrumb texture.

Pour the mixture into a large bowl, and stir in the caster sugar. Add the buttermilk and the vanilla extract to the mixture, stir to combine and knead slightly to bring together. Add the chocolate chips and bring the mixture together.

Sprinkle some extra flour onto a work surface and turn the dough out on to it. Gently roll it out, or press it down until it is about 4cm thick. Using a 5cm cutter, cut out the scones – you will have to re-roll the mixture a couple of times to get them all out of the mix.

Take the tray out of the oven, and arrange the scones on it. Brush the top of the scones with the beaten egg and bake for 10–12 minutes. Leave to cool for about 20 minutes.

Drizzle the melted milk chocolate over the scones and leave the chocolate to set. Serve the scones with clotted cream and chocolate spread.

WHITE CHOCOLATE RASPBERRY SCONES

♥ **Makes: 10**

Prep: 20 minutes
Bake: 10–12 minutes
Cool: 20 minutes
Lasts: 2–3 days, at room temperature

400g self-raising flour, plus extra
   for dusting
100g chilled unsalted butter, cubed
1 tsp baking powder
Pinch of salt
50g caster sugar
200ml full-fat milk
2 tbsp lemon juice
150g white chocolate chips or chunks
100g raspberries (fresh or frozen)
1 egg, beaten, for glazing
Raspberry jam and clotted cream,
   to serve

CUSTOMISE:
Frozen raspberries are often easier
to handle as there will be less
moisture in the dough, but fresh
work too! Alternatively, you can
use 15g freeze-dried raspberries.

You can swap the white chocolate
for milk or dark chocolate.

You can swap the raspberries for
other berries such as strawberries,
blackberries or blueberries.

You can add the zest of 1 lemon
for an extra fruity hit!

I absolutely love a classic scone, but why not add some flavours? White chocolate and raspberry is a winning combination – so inside a scone it's even better. Serve the scones with some raspberry jam and clotted cream and you have a perfect marriage of a dessert and scone.

Preheat the oven to 220°C/200°C fan and place a baking tray lined with parchment paper into the oven to preheat.

Tip the self-raising flour, butter, baking powder and salt into a food processor and pulse until the mixture resembles breadcrumbs. Alternatively, you can rub the mixture together with your fingertips to get the breadcrumb texture. Pour the mixture into a large bowl and stir in the caster sugar.

Heat the milk in a pan until it starts to steam – you want it to be warm, but not too hot. Add the warm milk and lemon juice to the bowl and stir with a spatula as it will be very wet at first. Mix the dough as little as possible until it just combines, then add the white chocolate chips and raspberries and fold through a few times.

Sprinkle some extra flour onto a work surface and turn the dough out onto it. Gently roll it out, or press it down until it is about 4cm thick. Using a 5cm cutter, cut out the scones – you will have to re-roll the mixture a couple of times to get them all out of the mix.

Take the tray out of the oven, and arrange the scones on it. Brush the top of the scones with the beaten egg and bake for 10–12 minutes. Leave to cool for about 20 minutes before serving with raspberry jam and clotted cream.

CHOCOLATE MUG CAKE

Serves: 1

Prep: 5 minutes
Cook: 1–2 minutes
Lasts: Best served fresh

45g self-raising flour
30g caster sugar
15g cocoa powder
1 tbsp sunflower or vegetable oil
4 tbsp full-fat milk
25g chocolate chips or chunks

When you've had a busy day, you want something sweet but you don't want all of the effort... you want something that is ready in just a few minutes, right? Mug cakes are the best solution to that problem. They are so quick to throw together, and are so delicious. You can make them practically any flavour you want, but a chocolate mug cake is my favourite by far.

Add the self-raising flour, caster sugar, cocoa powder, oil and milk to a large mug and mix with a fork or spoon until smooth. Add the chocolate chips and mix quickly again.

Microwave the mug cake for 1–1½ minutes, or until done. It will look wet on the top, but be cooked in the middle so be careful not to overdo it!

CUSTOMISE:
You can make these vegan by swapping the milk for a dairy-free milk such as almond, soya or oat milk.

The chocolate chips or chunks can be swapped for a heaped teaspoon of your favourite spread, such as a chocolate spread or nut spread.

The mug cake can be made plain by replacing the cocoa powder with the same amount of self-raising flour.

MICROWAVE CHOCOLATE COOKIES

Serves: 2

Prep: 5 minutes
Cook: 1–2 minutes
Lasts: Best served fresh

35g unsalted butter or baking spread
45g caster sugar or soft light brown
   sugar
1 egg (small or medium)
¼ tsp vanilla extract
90g plain flour
50–100g chocolate chips

Just like with a mug cake, sometimes you get a cookie craving. This delicious recipe creates two cookies in just 5 minutes. They are gooey, heavenly and you will want to make them again and again.

Add the butter to a bowl with the sugar and beat until smooth. Add the egg, vanilla extract and plain flour and mix with a spoon until smooth. Add the chocolate chips, and mix quickly again.

Split the mixture between 2 small mugs or ramekins. Microwave the cookies for 1 minute 10 seconds–1 minute 40 seconds, or until done. They will look wet on the top, but be cooked in the middle so be careful not to overdo it!

CUSTOMISE:

If you only want to eat one, you can cover the second with clingfilm and eat it the next day.

If you are only microwaving one cookie, reduce the time to 1 minute–1 minute 20 seconds.

You can make the cookie chocolate flavoured by replacing 15g of the plain flour with cocoa powder.

MACARONS

♥ Makes: 20–30

Prep: 2 hours
Cook: 18–20 minutes
Decorate: 30 minutes
Lasts: 5 days, in the fridge

200g icing sugar
100g ground almonds
100g egg whites (about 3 medium eggs)
75g caster sugar
½ tsp pink food colouring
1 tsp vanilla extract

FILLING:
50g unsalted butter, at room
   temperature
100g icing sugar
½ tsp pink food colouring

CUSTOMISE:
You can colour these whatever shade you like – I just chose pink!

You can flavour them with any flavouring you like as well, such as 1 tsp peppermint/orange/lemon/coffee extract.

The filling can be made any other colour you want, or can be flavoured. Or, instead of buttercream, you can fill the macarons with chocolate ganache (see page 190).

An afternoon tea classic. These pink vanilla macarons are filled with a dainty pink buttercream. They may look like an intimidating bake, but honestly they are worth the effort. They taste delicious, they are light, and you can customise them to whatever colours you prefer, or fill with other buttercream flavours. Heaven!

Sift the icing sugar and the ground almonds into a large bowl. It is very important that you sift it, as this will prevent any lumps. To be really sure you have no lumps, you can sift twice.

Put the egg whites into a separate large bowl and whisk them to stiff peaks. Start adding the caster sugar, 1 teaspoon at a time, until it is all incorporated, then whisk for a further minute. Add the food colouring and whisk until combined and you reach your desired colour.

Add the meringue mixture to the bowl of icing sugar and ground almonds, along with the vanilla extract. Carefully fold the mixture together, making sure that it is all combined. Use a rubber spatula to smooth the mixture around the edges of the bowl (this is called 'macaronage').

Transfer the mixture to a piping bag fitted with a small round tip (0.5cm) and line 2–3 baking trays with parchment paper. Carefully pipe the mixture onto the lined trays, making circles about 2cm in diameter. Space them well apart, as they will spread in the oven.

Once you have piped all your macarons, tap the trays onto the work surface 5 or 6 times to get any air bubbles out, and set aside for 1 hour to form a skin. Towards the end of the hour, preheat your oven to 150°C/130°C fan.

Bake the macarons for 18–20 minutes. You can check they are done by carefully lifting off one of the shells – it should come off cleanly. Remove from the oven, and leave to cool fully on the trays while you make the filling.

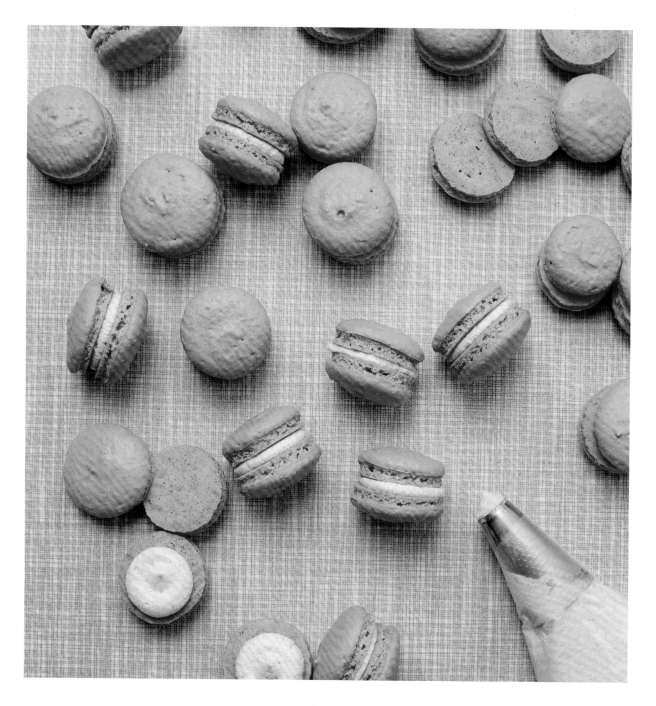

Beat the butter on its own so it is smooth. Add the icing sugar and pink food colouring and beat again until fluffy.

Carefully peel the macarons off the parchment paper and then pipe a small amount of buttercream on to one macaron, then sandwich with another macaron. Put them into the fridge for the buttercream to set for an hour or so, and then enjoy.

CHOCOLATE MACARONS

♥ Makes: 20–30

Prep: 2 hours
Cook: 18–20 minutes
Decorate: 30 minutes
Lasts: 5+ days, in the fridge

185g icing sugar
15g cocoa powder
100g ground almonds
100g egg whites (about 3 medium eggs)
75g caster sugar
½ tsp vanilla extract

FILLING:
100g dark chocolate, finely chopped
100ml double cream

CUSTOMISE:
You can flavour the macarons with any flavouring you like, such as 1 tsp peppermint/orange/lemon/coffee extract.

The shells freeze well for 3+ months if you would like to make them ahead.

If you do not want to fill the shells straight away, store them in the fridge until you are ready to fill.

Make a white chocolate ganache with 150g white chocolate and 50ml double cream.

Make a milk chocolate ganache with 125g milk chocolate and 65ml double cream.

An afternoon tea is full of dainty delicious treats that I love. I am obsessed with anything chocolate however, so baking chocolate macarons is perfection. These macaron shells are so simple to make!

Sift the icing sugar, cocoa powder and ground almonds into a large bowl.

Whisk the egg whites in a separate large bowl to form stiff peaks. Start adding the caster sugar, 1 teaspoon at a time, until it is all incorporated, then continue whisking for a further minute. Add this meringue mixture to the icing sugar, cocoa powder and ground almonds, along with the vanilla extract.

Fold the mixture carefully but making sure that it is all combined. Use a spatula to press the mixture around the edges of the bowl to smooth it out.

Line 2–3 baking trays with parchment paper, then transfer the macaron mixture to a piping bag fitted with a small round tip (0.5cm). Carefully pipe the mixture onto the lined trays in circles about 2cm in diameter, spacing them apart as they will spread in the oven.

Once piped, tap the trays on the work surface 5–6 times to get any air bubbles out, and leave on the side for 1 hour to form a skin. Towards the end of the hour, preheat the oven to 150°C/130°C fan.

Bake the macarons for 18–20 minutes. You can check they are done by carefully lifting off one of the shells – it should come off cleanly. Remove from the oven, and leave to cool fully while you make the filling.

Add the dark chocolate to a bowl. Heat the double cream in a pan until it is just starting to boil, then pour it over the dark chocolate. Leave it to sit for 5 minutes, and then stir together. Leave again for 5 minutes to cool slightly, and then transfer to a piping bag and pipe a small amount into the middle of a macaron shell, then sandwich with another shell. Put the filled macarons into the fridge for an hour or so for the ganache to set, then enjoy.

CHOCOLATE TWISTS

♥ **Makes: 10**

Prep: 15 minutes
Cook: 12 minutes
Lasts: 2 days (but best served fresh)

300–400g puff pastry
150g chocolate spread
1 egg, beaten, for glazing

I love pastry and I love croissants, so this quick and easy treat satisfies all of my chocolate pastry cravings. Puff pastry + chocolate spread = one of the most delicious bakes ever.

Preheat the oven to 220°C/200°C fan and line 2 baking sheets with parchment paper.

Roll out the puff pastry to form a large rectangle that is about 3mm thick. Cut the pastry into two equal pieces. Carefully spread the chocolate spread onto one of the pieces of puff pastry, then add the second piece of puff pastry on top. Cut this into 1cm strips.

Twist each strip a few times to create a twist, then place on the lined baking trays. Once they are all twisted, lightly brush the tops of the twists with the beaten egg. Bake for about 12 minutes, or until a lovely a golden brown. Leave to cool, then enjoy!

Image overleaf →

CUSTOMISE:
Instead of egg, you can use milk to brush over the pastry before baking.

You can use any flavour chocolate spread, or switch to a different type of spread!

You can add up to 100g chopped nuts or fruits – sprinkle on top of the chocolate spread before adding the second layer of pastry.

These can be frozen raw and baked when required.

Instead of twists, you can roll the pastry up and cut into rounds and have swirls!

CHOCOLATE CHEESECAKE CRÊPES

♥ Makes: 8

Prep: 45 minutes
Cook: 15 minutes
Lasts: Best served fresh

225g plain flour
25g cocoa powder
3 eggs, plus 1 egg yolk
550ml milk (semi-skimmed or full-fat)
25g melted butter or 25ml sunflower
   oil, for frying

CHEESECAKE FILLING:
250g full-fat soft cheese/
   mascarpone
2 tbsp icing sugar
1 tbsp cocoa powder

TO SERVE:
Biscuit crumbs
Chocolate sauce
Fresh berries

CUSTOMISE:
You can add 2 tbsp of salted caramel sauce to make the filling caramel flavoured.

If you prefer plain crêpes, remove the cocoa powder and use a total of 250g plain flour.

You can freeze unfilled pancakes, stacked with parchment paper in between, for a later date!

When we think of crêpes or pancakes we naturally think of Pancake Day, but when you can make something as deliciously light yet chocolatey as these chocolate cheesecake crêpes, you will want to make them year round! They are so easy and perfect to customise to your personal taste.

Put the plain flour and cocoa powder into a bowl and make a well in the middle. Add the eggs and egg yolk to the well and slowly whisk together, then gradually pour in the milk, whisking all the time. Keep whisking until the mixture is smooth and the consistency of single cream. Leave the mixture to sit for 15–30 minutes or so.

Place a crêpe or frying pan over a medium heat, add 1 teaspoon of melted butter or sunflower oil and use kitchen paper to rub over the pan to grease it. Add a small ladleful of pancake mixture to the pan and swirl until the base of the pan is coated evenly. Cook for 1–2 minutes, or until the underside of the crêpe is cooked through, and then flip and cook the other side.

Remove from the pan and transfer to a warm plate to keep warm. Repeat until the batter is all used up, stacking the crêpes between layers of parchment paper to keep them separate. Keep warm in a low oven while you make the filling.

Beat together the soft cheese with the icing sugar and cocoa powder until smooth and creamy.

When you are ready to serve, get a crêpe, and add 1 heaped tablespoon of cheesecake filling to it. Sprinkle over some crushed biscuits, and fold the crêpe into a quarter shape. Add a drizzle of chocolate sauce and some crushed biscuits to serve, along with some delicious fresh berries!

I adore baking cakes, cheesecakes, cupcakes, desserts and so on but some of the most popular treats I have ever made on my blog are the sweets. My readers love them, and so do I. These are easy to make, and everyone loves the fact that they make a lot of smaller servings.

Whether you are wanting to make chocolate bark or honeycomb (which are both just so much fun to do), or go down the route of making fudge, marshmallows or truffles, there are so many sweets to choose from and they are all utterly scrumptious!

Fudge can be made in two ways: the classic technique where you boil your ingredients together and measure the temperature with a thermometer and you get the crumbly delicious fudge flavour, or the easy way with condensed milk and chocolate, which you can create in no time at all. Both are amazing, and you'll find both in this book!

Truffles are just as delicious and the perfect indulgent bite-sized treat. I adore creating truffles because they are so much fun to make – getting messy and covered in chocolate is all part of the process. So whether you fancy a classic chocolate ganache truffle or want to experiment with a cheesecake one, they're all here in this chapter alongside lots of other amazing flavours.

Marshmallows are an iconic hot chocolate topping when the weather is cold, but making your own is just the best. They are pillowy, soft and sweet treats that you will absolutely adore.

I'll always love making sweets as they are just so exciting and delicious, and I'm sure you will love making them too!

MY TOP TIPS FOR SWEETS:

1 When making a recipe with condensed milk, make sure to use full-fat sweetened condensed milk and not the light version as this can prevent the mixture setting. Also, make sure not to use evaporated milk.

2 When making a recipe with dark chocolate, it is important to use one that has at least 70% cocoa solids to help the mixture taste its best.

3 Cream is a key ingredient and make sure you use double rather than single cream as you need the fat content.

4 Be patient when it comes to a recipe setting – the freezer can help speed things up but it will set fine in the fridge too!

CHOCOLATE BARK

Serves: 10

Prep: 10 minutes
Cool: 2 hours
Lasts: 2+ weeks, in the fridge

400g milk chocolate
200g white chocolate

DECORATION IDEAS:
100g chocolate sweets
50g mini marshmallows
Sprinkles
Chocolate curls
Freeze-dried raspberries

This quick, homemade chocolate bark is a favourite on my blog and can be adapted to whatever you like and love. You can use this recipe to create a quick chocolate treat for your family, or it can be used to decorate other bakes! It's so easily customised it is amazing.

Line a large rectangular baking tray (23 x 33cm) with parchment paper.

Carefully melt each chocolate in a separate heatproof bowl, until smooth. I do this in the microwave but you could set the bowls over a pan of just simmering water (bain-marie).

Pour the melted milk chocolate onto the lined tray, and spread until even. Spoon the melted white chocolate on top of the milk chocolate, and swirl together with a skewer, then sprinkle over your chosen toppings. I use chocolate sweets, mini marshmallows, sprinkles, chocolate curls and freeze-dried raspberries.

Leave the chocolate bark to set in the fridge until solid, then break up into shards and enjoy.

CUSTOMISE:
You can switch the chocolate to whatever you prefer – use all one flavour, or three, it's up to you!

You can halve the mixture if you want to make less.

You can leave out the toppings or go all out and use even more. Whatever you want goes!

HONEYCOMB

Serves: 8

Prep: 10 minutes
Cool: 2 hours
Lasts: 2+ weeks, at room temperature

175g caster sugar
100g golden syrup
2 tsp bicarbonate of soda

Honeycomb is something that probably comes to mind when you think of bees, or honey, but it's such a delicious sweet treat. It's so simple to make, and looks like a science experiment when you are creating it. Three ingredients create something that is perfect to flavour so many bakes with... cakes, cheesecakes, cupcakes, or more!

Line a large, deep baking tray with parchment paper – I use one that is 23 x 33cm.

Pour the caster sugar and golden syrup into a large pan and place over a low-medium heat, stirring until the sugar has dissolved and the texture turns gooey. Turn the heat up to medium and simmer until the mixture turns a golden brown colour.

Remove from the heat and immediately add the bicarbonate of soda (don't be tempted to use baking powder instead – it won't work!). Whisk it in straight away and watch it rise and bubble in the pan. The less you whisk the better. Pour into the tray and leave it to set and cool.

Once set, break into pieces, and enjoy.

Image overleaf →

CUSTOMISE:
Melt 200–300g chocolate and use to coat the pieces of honeycomb to make it a chocolate bar!
You can use dark, milk or white chocolate.

Instead of golden syrup, you can use a clear honey.

TRIPLE CHOCOLATE TRUFFLES

♥ Makes: 25

Prep: 30 minutes
Set: 2 hours
Decorate: 1 hour
Lasts: 1 week, in the fridge

WHITE CHOCOLATE LAYER:
225g white chocolate, chopped
75ml double cream

MILK CHOCOLATE LAYER:
200g milk chocolate, chopped
100ml double cream

DARK CHOCOLATE LAYER:
150g dark chocolate, chopped
150ml double cream

DECORATION:
200g chocolate of your choice, melted

These quick chocolate truffles use just four ingredients – a mixture of white, milk and dark chocolate and double cream create an absolute wonder of deliciousness!

Line a 20cm square tin with parchment paper or clingfilm.

Add each chocolate to a separate bowl.

Pour all of the double cream into a small pan and heat until just before boiling point. It should be steaming, and bubbling slightly around the edge of the pan, but not boiling. Pour the hot cream over the chocolates, making sure to stick to the correct amounts (pour it into a measuring jug first). Let each bowl sit for 5 minutes to let the cream melt the chocolate. After 5 minutes, stir each bowl until the mixture is smooth. If any lumps of chocolate remain, briefly heat in the microwave until smooth or return to a pan to melt.

Pour each type of chocolate into the lined tin and layer, or swirl together, then place into the freezer and freeze until solid.

Carefully remove the mixture from the tray and cut into small squares, then dunk each square into the melted chocolate. Place on to a lined tray and chill in the fridge for about 30 minutes to make sure the chocolate sets.

CUSTOMISE:
You can set the mixture and use a melon baller to create round truffles if you prefer.

You can coat the set truffle squares in 75g cocoa powder if you like.

IRISH CREAM LIQUEUR FUDGE

Makes: 25 pieces

Prep: 15 minutes
Set: 5–6 hours
Lasts: 2+ weeks, in the fridge

600g dark chocolate
397g tin condensed milk
125ml Irish cream liqueur

When I think of Irish cream liqueur, I think of Christmas and fun evenings with my friends and family... but cooking with it is a revelation. This simple three-ingredient fudge from my blog is incredibly easy to make, and so utterly delicious!

Line an 18 x 25cm rectangular tin or a 20cm square tin with parchment paper.

Put the dark chocolate and condensed milk into a heavy-based pan and melt over a low heat, stirring often so that the chocolate does not catch on the bottom.

Once melted, pour in the Irish cream liqueur and stir through until combined. Pour into the tin and smooth over the mixture. Chill in the fridge to set for at least 5–6 hours, or overnight.

Once set, remove from the tin and cut into 25 squares. Return to the fridge for another couple of hours to finish setting, if required.

CUSTOMISE:

If you want to use just milk chocolate, you'll need 800g.

Any cream liqueur will work – and any flavoured one too!

You can freeze the fudge to make it set quicker.

Try using this mixture on top of a brownie – bake a brownie and allow to cool fully. Pour the fudge mixture on top and then set for at least 5 hours.

LEMON MERINGUE FUDGE

Makes: 25 pieces

Prep: 15 minutes
Set: 3–4+ hours
Lasts: 2+ weeks, in the fridge

600g white chocolate
397g tin condensed milk
2 tsp lemon extract
½ tsp yellow food colouring
6–8 shop-bought meringues, crushed

Lemon meringue is a dessert we all know and love – it's sweet, sour and always moreish. However, in fudge form, it's even better! This simple sweet treat has been so poplar on my blog, it had to have a place here.

Line a 18 x 25cm rectangular tin or a 20cm square tin with parchment paper.

Put the white chocolate, condensed milk and lemon extract into a heavy-based pan and melt over a low heat, stirring often, so that the chocolate does not catch on the bottom. Remove from the heat, add the yellow food colouring and stir.

Pour in most of the crushed meringues and quickly stir through, then pour into the prepared tin and smooth over the mixture. Sprinkle on the rest of the meringues and press into the top of the fudge. Chill in the fridge to set for at least 3–4 hours, or overnight.

Once set, remove from the tin and cut into 25 squares. Return to the fridge for another couple of hours to finish setting, if required.

CUSTOMISE:
You can use lemon zest in place of the extract – you will need about 2 lemons.

You can leave out the meringue to make a lemon fudge.

You can flavour the fudge with any other flavouring you like – orange, peppermint, and coffee all work well.

MALT CHOCOLATE FUDGE

Makes: 25 pieces

Prep: 15 minutes
Set: 4+ hours
Lasts: 2+ weeks, in the fridge

250g dark chocolate
250g milk chocolate
397g tin condensed milk
75g malt drink powder (I use Horlicks)
200g chocolate malt balls (I use Maltesers)

For this fudge I decided to use dark and milk chocolate, but you can easily just use milk, or just dark. I also used malt drink powder to make it a bit more malt chocolate like. It's super chocolatey, sweet and absolutely heavenly. Think of it as a cosy fudge, which you will want to make again and again.

Line a 18 x 25cm rectangular tin or a 20cm square tin with parchment paper.

Put the dark chocolate, milk chocolate and condensed milk into a heavy-based pan and melt over a low heat, stirring often so that the chocolate does not catch on the bottom.

Once melted, add the malt drink powder and stir through until combined. Finally, fold through most of the chocolate malt balls. Pour into the tin and smooth over the mixture. Add the remaining chocolate malt balls and press into the top of the fudge. Chill in the fridge to set for at least 3–4 hours, or overnight.

Once set, remove from the tin and cut into 25 squares. Return to the fridge for another couple of hours to finish setting, if required.

CUSTOMISE:
If you want to use just dark chocolate, you'll need 400g.

If you want to use just milk chocolate, you'll need 600g.

MILLIONAIRE'S FUDGE

 Makes: 40 pieces

Prep: 30 minutes
Set: 5+ hours
Lasts: 1 week, in the fridge

350g condensed milk
275g soft light brown sugar
175g unsalted butter
3 tbsp golden syrup
1 tsp vanilla extract
300g white chocolate, chopped
200g digestive biscuits, chopped

TOPPING:
200g milk chocolate, melted

CUSTOMISE:
To create the caramel taste this recipe works best with white chocolate in the main fudge mixture but you can replace with milk or dark chocolate if you prefer.

You can also use any flavour chocolate to coat the fudge.

Leave out the digestive biscuits if you just want to make a caramel fudge.

You can add ½–1 tsp sea salt if you want a salted caramel fudge – add this when you add the white chocolate.

When thinking about millionaire's shortbread you think of caramel, biscuit and chocolate... so why can't this translate into a fudge as well? A deliciously smooth, white-chocolate-based caramel fudge dotted with biscuit, coated in a smooth and luscious milk chocolate!

Line a 23cm square tin or a 18 x 25cm rectangular tin with parchment paper.

Add the condensed milk, soft light brown sugar, butter and golden syrup to a large pan and melt over a low heat, stirring constantly, until the sugar dissolves and all of the ingredients combine.

Turn up the heat and let the mixture simmer, while still stirring, until the mixture has visibly thickened. You can test the temperature if you have a thermometer – it should have reached 110°C. Once thickened, take the pan off the heat and add the vanilla extract and white chocolate. Stir the chocolate into the fudge mixture until it has melted and the mixture is smooth. Pour in the chopped digestive biscuits and stir again.

Pour into the tin and smooth over the mixture. Chill in the fridge to set for at least 3–4 hours, or overnight.

Once set, remove from the tin and cut into 40 squares, then coat each square in melted milk chocolate, and place onto a lined tray. Return to the fridge for another couple of hours to finish setting.

PEPPERMINT CREAMS

❤ **Makes: 25 pieces**

Prep: 25 minutes
Set: 3 hours
Lasts: 2+ weeks, in the fridge

100g chocolate (white, milk or dark)
275g icing sugar
1 egg white
½ tsp peppermint extract

I will always choose something minty if it is an option because I absolutely love it – peppermint creams are an easy way of making something that looks like you spent a lot of time on it, but in reality they are easy to make and so easy to eat! These make beautiful little homemade edible gifts for people, or just for you if you are in the mood for something delicious.

Add your chocolate of choice to a heatproof bowl and melt in the microwave in short bursts. Alternatively, set the bowl over a pan of simmering water (bain-marie) and melt until smooth. Let the chocolate cool for about 5 minutes.

Sift the icing sugar into a medium bowl. Gradually add the egg white and peppermint extract and mix well each time until the icing sugar forms a dough that isn't sticky. If you find it too sticky, add more icing sugar to compensate.

Knead the dough slightly so you know it is smooth, then divide it into 25 balls. Flatten each one into a disc shape and place onto a tray lined with parchment paper.

Carefully dip half of each of the peppermint creams into the cooled melted chocolate, and place back onto the lined tray. Leave the peppermint creams to set at room temperature until the chocolate is solid.

CUSTOMISE:

You can use the same recipe to create a different flavour, such as almond, lemon, vanilla, orange – any extract you fancy!

You can use any flavour chocolate to coat the peppermint creams, and you can double the amount to fully coat of them in chocolate.

EDIBLE COOKIE DOUGH

♥ **Makes: 25 pieces**

Prep: 15 minutes
Bake: 5 minutes
Set: 1+ hours
Lasts: 2+ weeks, in the fridge

250g plain flour
175g unsalted butter, at room
    temperature
225g soft light brown sugar
1 tsp vanilla extract
50ml full-fat milk
250g chocolate, chopped

Whenever I make cookies I always think the cookie dough looks completely and utterly delicious... and I just can't help eating it! Of course, eating raw cookie dough isn't the best, which makes this edible cookie dough so good! It's all you need when you just want a small bite of something incredibly delicious.

Preheat the oven to 200°C/180°C fan.

Spread the plain flour out on a baking tray and bake for 5 minutes. Once baked, leave to cool fully.

Put the butter and soft light brown sugar in a bowl and beat until light and fluffy. Add the vanilla extract and cooled plain flour and beat again, then add the milk and chopped chocolate and mix until the chocolate is evenly distributed.

You can press the cookie dough into a lined tray, and then portion, or roll the cookie dough into bite-sized balls. Chill the in the fridge for at least 1 hour, then enjoy.

CUSTOMISE:
The cookie dough can be made into cookie dough truffles by coating in melted chocolate: melt 200g dark, milk or white chocolate and use to coat the balls, then set in the fridge until solid.

The chocolate that you add to the cookie dough can be any flavour you like!

VANILLA MARSHMALLOWS

♥ **Makes: 25 pieces**

Prep: 20 minutes
Cook: 20 minutes
Set: 5–6 hours
Lasts: 2+ weeks, at room temperature

450g caster sugar
75g liquid glucose
115ml water
20g powdered gelatine
3 tbsp boiling water
2 egg whites
2 tsp vanilla extract
unsalted butter, for greasing
** (optional)**
150g icing sugar
50g cornflour

CUSTOMISE:
If you would like to flavour your marshmallows any other flavour, you can swap the vanilla for orange, lemon, peppermint or almond extract.

You can coat the marshmallows in 200g melted chocolate. Leave the coated marshmallows to set on a lined tray.

Marshmallows are a great treat to have on top of a hot chocolate or as part of s'mores. When you make your own they are incredible – pillowy soft, utterly fantastic, and so much fun to make.

Add the caster sugar, liquid glucose and water to a large pan. Mix briefly before placing over a medium-high heat and heat until the mixture comes to a boil. Try not to stir the sugar mixture, but you can swirl the pan slightly to move the mixture about.

While the sugar mixture is heating, put the powdered gelatine and boiling water into a small bowl and mix to combine. Set aside while you return to the sugar mixture.

Using a sugar thermometer, heat the sugar mixture until it reaches 120°C. As it starts to reach this temperature, put the egg whites into a large bowl and start to whisk to stiff peaks – this is easiest to do in a stand mixer.

Once the temperature has been reached, and the egg whites are in stiff peaks, carefully and slowly pour the syrup into the egg whites while mixing on a medium speed. The syrup should run into the egg whites as a drizzle, and towards the edges of the bowl rather than the centre of the mixture.

Pour in the vanilla extract. Continue to whisk once all of the syrup has been added for about 3 minutes. Carefully pour in the melted gelatine mix, and whisk again for a further minute.

While the mixture is whisking, grease an 20–23cm square tin with butter, or line with parchment paper. Carefully pour the marshmallow mixture into the tin. Sift a third of the icing sugar over the top and leave the mixture to set in the tin for 5–6 hours at room temperature.

Once the marshmallow is set, dust a work surface with the remaining icing sugar mixed with the cornflour. Turn the marshmallows out and portion using a sharp and lightly oiled knife. Toss the cut marshmallows in the dusting powder so they are covered, and enjoy!

CHEESECAKE TRUFFLES

♥ **Makes: 25 pieces**

Prep: 30 minutes
Bake: 10 minutes
Chill: 3+ hours
Lasts: 2+ weeks, in the fridge

300g full-fat soft cheese, chilled
50g icing sugar
175g biscuit crumbs, finely crushed

DECORATION:
200g milk chocolate, melted
50g biscuit crumbs, finely crushed

As you will have gathered by now, cheesecake is one of my favourite things in the world… These truffles combine that sweet cheesecake topping with crunchy biscuit to create a fun alternative to a homemade sweet. Fill with your favourite biscuit and create something wonderful!

Add the soft cheese to a bowl and mix briefly until smooth before adding the icing sugar and mixing again briefly until combined.

Pour the crushed biscuit crumbs into the mix and fold together until combined. Refrigerate the mixture for at least 2 hours.

Take the chilled mixture out of the fridge and scoop into truffle shapes using 2 teaspoons or a melon baller, then place onto a tray lined with parchment paper. Return the truffles to the fridge for another hour, or the freezer for 30 minutes.

To decorate the truffles, carefully dip each truffle into the melted milk chocolate and place back onto the lined tray. You can use small spoons or forks to help with this. Once dipped, sprinkle the tops with the extra crushed biscuits.

CUSTOMISE:
You can use any biscuit you want – cookies and cream, speculoos and digestive biscuits all work brilliantly!

You can coat the truffles in any flavour chocolate you want instead of the milk chocolate.

Mascarpone can be used in place of the full-fat soft cheese if you prefer a sweeter flavour.

INDEX

FOLLOWER REQUESTS

CONVERSION CHARTS

OVEN TEMPERATURES

110°C	90°C fan	225°F	Gas Mark ¼
130°C	110°C fan	250°F	Gas Mark ½
140°C	120°C fan	275°F	Gas Mark 1
150°C	130°C fan	300°F	Gas Mark 2
170°C	150°C fan	325°F	Gas Mark 3
180°C	160°C fan	350°F	Gas Mark 4
190°C	170°C fan	375°F	Gas Mark 5
200°C	180°C fan	400°F	Gas Mark 6
220°C	200°C fan	425°F	Gas Mark 7

WEIGHT CONVERSIONS
(METRIC VS IMPERIAL)*

15g	½oz
25g	1oz
40g	1½oz
50g	2oz
75g	3oz
100g	4oz
150g	5oz
175g	6oz
200g	7oz
225g	8oz
250g	9oz
275g	10oz
350g	12oz
375g	13oz
400g	14oz
425g	15oz
450g	1lb
550g	1¼lb
675g	1½lb
900g	2lb
1.5kg	3lb

VOLUME CONVERSIONS
(METRIC VS IMPERIAL)

25ml	1fl oz
50ml	2fl oz
85ml	3fl oz
150ml	5fl oz (¼ pint)
300ml	10fl oz (½ pint)
450ml	15fl oz (¾ pint)
600ml	1 pint
700ml	1¼ pints
900ml	1½ pints
1 litres	1¾ pints
1.2 litres	2 pints
1.25 litres	2¼ pints
1.5 litres	2½ pints
1.6 litres	2¾ pints
1.75 litres	3 pints
1.8 litres	3¼ pints
2 litres	3½ pints

*28.35g = 1oz but the measurements in this table have been rounded up or down to make conversions easier.

ACKNOWLEDGEMENTS

To my Mum, Dad and Brother... thank you for letting me take over your kitchen and for letting me leave it in a mess for so many years when I started this journey. I know sometimes having to wipe chocolate or cake mixture off the wall wasn't what you had in mind, but thank you so much for letting me do what I love. Thank you for helping me find happiness in baking and for supporting me throughout. I never really knew what I wanted to do when I grew up, and going to cookery school and starting a blog wasn't what any of us expected, but I couldn't have done it without you. Thank you for letting me choose. Thank you for teaching me to only do what makes me happy. I love you all so dearly.

To my friends, thank you for letting me be myself around you all. All I ever talk about is my blog, or cake, or something to do with baking - but I know I can count on your support whenever I need it. You have always been the best advice givers, and you are the best friends that I could have asked for.

To Ivy, my Gran, you may have passed away when I was little, but I trust that I got my love for baking and cooking from you. Thank you for making my pink first birthday cake. Thank you for writing down so many recipes that we can still make now, so many years later.

To my readers and followers, thank you for supporting me in my journey from the very beginning. You are in every single corner of the world, and I couldn't have done this without you. From baking my recipes, sharing everything with your friends and family, and for helping me create this delicious little world. It will never fail to amaze me how supportive you all are.

Thank you.

Jane x

Published in 2021 by Ebury Press an imprint of Ebury Publishing,
20 Vauxhall Bridge Road,
London SW1V 2SA

Ebury Press is part of the Penguin Random House group of companies
whose addresses can be found at global.penguinrandomhouse.com

First published by Ebury Press in 2021

www.penguin.co.uk

A CIP catalogue record for this book is available from the British Library

ISBN 9781529109429

Project Editor: Sam Crisp
Text Design: Louise Evans
Photography: Ellis Parrinder
Food Styling: Sarah Hardy
Prop Styling: Hannah Wilkinson

Colour reproduction by AltaImage

Printed and bound in China by C&C Offset Printing Co., Ltd

The authorised representative in the EEA is Penguin Random House
Ireland, Morrison Chambers, 32 Nassau Street, Dublin D02 YH68.

Penguin Random House is committed to a sustainable future for our
business, our readers and our planet. This book is made from Forest
Stewardship Council® certified paper.